Exploring Gun Use
in America

Titles in the series

Exploring Gun Use in America

VOLUME 4

Public Opinion

GREENWOOD PRESS
Westport, Connecticut · London

Library of Congress Cataloging-in-Publication Data

Exploring gun use in America / Creative Media Applications.
      p. cm. — (Middle school reference)
    Includes bibliographical references and index.
    Contents: v. 1. The second amendment — v. 2. The firearms industry —
v. 3. Children and guns — v. 4. Public opinion.
    ISBN 0–313–32896–X (alk. paper: set) — ISBN 0–313–32897–8 (alk. paper: vol. 1) —
ISBN 0–313–32898–6 (alk. paper: vol. 2) — ISBN 0–313–32899–4 (alk. paper: vol. 3) —
ISBN 0–313–32900–1 (alk. paper: vol. 4)
      1. Gun control — United States. 2. Firearms — Law and legislation — United States.
      3. Gun control — United States — Public opinion. 4. Public opinion — United States.
      I. Creative Media Applications. II. Series.
    HV7436.E94   2004
    363.33′0973 — dc22   2003067750

British Library Cataloguing in Publication Data is available.

Library of Congress Catalog Card Number: 2003067750
ISBN: 0–313–32896–X (set)
       0–313–32897–8 (vol. 1)
       0–313–32898–6 (vol. 2)
       0–313–32899–4 (vol. 3)
       0–313–32900–1 (vol. 4)

First published in 2004

Greenwood Press, 88 Post Road West, Westport, CT 06881
An imprint of Greenwood Publishing Group, Inc.
www.greenwood.com

Printed in the United States of America

The paper used in this book complies with the
Permanent Paper Standard issued by the National
Information Standards Organization (Z39.48–1984).

10 9 8 7 6 5 4 3 2 1

A Creative Media Applications, Inc. Production
WRITER: Mathew Kachur
DESIGN AND PRODUCTION: Alan Barnett, Inc.
EDITOR: Matt Levine
COPYEDITOR: Laurie Lieb
PROOFREADER: Betty Pessagno
INDEXER: Nara Wood
ASSOCIATED PRESS PHOTO RESEARCHER: Yvette Reyes
CONSULTANT: Eugene Volokh, Professor of Law, UCLA School of Law

PHOTO CREDITS:
AP/Wide World Photographs *pages:* viii, 1, 4, 6, 9, 10, 13, 14, 17, 19, 21, 22, 25, 26, 29, 30, 33, 34, 37, 38, 43, 47, 49, 50, 53, 54, 57,
    60, 62, 65, 66, 68, 71, 75, 76, 78, 82, 97, 98, 101, 103, 104, 113, 115, 116
© Bettmann/CORBIS *pages:* 3, 73, 89, 93
© Scott Houston/Corbis *page:* 44, 90, 119
© Roy Morsch/CORBIS *page:* 86
© Reuters/CORBIS *pages:* 95, 108, 110, 120
© Royalty-Free/CORBIS *page:* 107

Table of Contents

INTRODUCTION

Because guns are so common in America, they play a significant part in American life. There are anywhere from 65 million to 250 million guns in the United States; a common estimate is 200 million. A survey in March 2001 indicated that guns are present in about four out of every ten households in the United States. Just over a quarter of Americans own a firearm, although gun ownership is much higher among adult men (49 percent) than adult women (12 percent).

Millions of Americans use guns for hunting, target shooting, and self-defense. Estimates of defensive gun use—the times that a firearm is used in the United States to protect a person from danger—range from 60,000 to 2.5 million a year. At the same time, guns are also used to commit crimes. The Department of Justice's National Crime Victimization Survey (NCVS) found that in 2000, more than half a million victims of serious violent crimes (rape and sexual assault, robbery, and aggravated assault) faced an offender with a firearm. The Federal Bureau of Investigation (FBI) estimated that two-thirds of the 15,517 murders in 2000 were committed with firearms. No matter which figures are emphasized, no one would dispute that firearms are an important part of many Americans' identity and lifestyle.

> **FAST FACT**
>
> In a 2001 poll, the main reason given for gun ownership was hunting (49 percent), followed by protection (26 percent), target and sport shooting (8 percent), and collecting as a hobby (4 percent).

Guns and Public Opinion

The Second Amendment to the U.S. Constitution states, "A well regulated militia, being necessary to the security of a free State, the right of the people to keep and bear arms,

An EMS crew stands by to lift a teenage victim of an accidental shooting at Fair Park High School in Shreveport, Louisiana, in 2003. Gun ownership is a hotly debated topic because people's emotion over tragic situations like this one can often be at odds with their political beliefs.

shall not be infringed." Although this amendment deals specifically with the right of Americans to own firearms, the meaning of its words is greatly disputed. This is because the question of gun ownership in America is not just historical in nature. Rather, it involves current public opinion—"What do the American people want regarding firearms and gun regulations at this particular moment?" It might seem to be a fairly straightforward question, but it is not.

The United States is a democracy. This means that the people have a voice in choosing not only their leaders but also the policies and laws that will affect their everyday lives. Unlike a dictatorship, in which one person or a small group makes decisions, the American government responds, at least to some degree, to the desires of its citizens. In 1859, Abraham Lincoln, speaking in Ohio on the issue of slavery in the United States, noted, "Public opinion in this country is everything."

Americans can make their views known, thereby affecting public policy, in several ways. They can vote for officials to represent them; those with the most votes will then stand for the majority's view of which laws the people would like to see passed. Citizens can write letters to newspapers or directly to their elected leaders, who will presumably take the letter-writers' opinions into account when deciding on new laws. In addition to freedom of speech, the U.S. Constitution grants citizens the right to assemble freely and hold demonstrations or parades to popularize their causes. In some cases, known as *referendums* or *initiatives*, they can even vote directly on laws. Public opinion polls also indicate to politicians where the people stand on any position.

Taken all together, the American public seems to send mixed signals regarding guns and gun regulations. While polls consistently indicate a high level of support for increased control of firearms, this has not been reflected in either the election of public officials or the passage of laws. In addition, the public's attitude toward guns varies from year to year, affected by incidents such as assassinations, school shootings, the Oklahoma City bombing of 1995, the terrorist attack of September 11, 2001, variations in the crime rate, and the perceived success or failure of gun control laws.

An Emotional Issue

Because the use of guns potentially involves life and death, it will always remain an emotionally charged issue. Consider the following stories.

In August 2003 in Brooklyn, New York, a nine-year-old boy accidentally shot his three-year-old cousin in the head with a revolver. The boy found the weapon hidden under the bedroom mattress belonging to his seventeen-year-old brother. He was playing with it when it went off and hit the toddler, who was seriously injured.

In January 2002 in Niagara Falls, New York, a shopkeeper defended himself against a robber by using a hidden gun. The robber entered the store holding a knife, demanded money, and lunged over the counter, cutting the shopkeeper on the nose. The shopkeeper then grabbed a shotgun from behind the counter and the suspect fled the store.

It is almost impossible not to sympathize with both the three-year-old boy and the shopkeeper, thus—by extension—taking a position on gun ownership. Because there are millions of firearms in the United States, there is no shortage of these types of examples. Both defenders of gun use and supporters of gun regulations skillfully use these stories to attempt to sway public opinion. For both sides, the stakes are extremely high. For gun advocates, firearms are a basic part of American freedom and individual self-defense. For gun control sponsors, unregulated firearms increase the number of crimes, suicides, and accidental injuries and deaths. These two points of view are difficult to reconcile, and the battle between them continually plays out in both state and national politics, and in the realm of American public opinion. As the great women's suffrage leader Carrie Chapman Catt said, "No written law has ever been more binding than unwritten custom supported by popular opinion."

CHAPTER 1

Guns and Polls

Because the United States is a democracy, the opinions of Americans are important. Elections usually involve voting for or against a person who has taken a variety of positions that the voter may or may not agree with. When politicians are elected to public office, however, it's very difficult to determine which of their positions led to the voters' support. Except for rare referendums or initiatives on specific issues, votes for particular politicians may involve their stance on tax cuts, foreign policy, or any number of topics.

On the other hand, elected officials support or oppose laws in response to many stimuli, including personal principle, donations of money for campaign contributions, positive or negative publicity, and letters written by voters directly to the politician. Since the second half of the twentieth century, public opinion polls have played a crucial role in tilting an elected representative toward one position or another. A *poll* is a survey of public opinion taken by asking questions of a small group of people, or sample. The answers of this sample, if chosen carefully enough, are supposedly representative of the whole population. Polls try to find or create a sample of people (known as *respondents*) whose opinions would be exactly the same as those that would have been obtained if it were somehow possible to interview every adult American in the nation. Polls influence policy makers and politicians to pass or reject legislation based on its popularity with "the people." All sides of the gun regulation debate use poll results to support their position and attack that of their opponents.

Some Problems with Polls

Most Americans generally trust the results of national public opinion polls by companies such as Gallup, Harris, ABC News, or the National Opinion Research Center, although they often disagree with the principles on which the polls are based. In one recent Gallup "poll on polls," respondents said that polls generally do a good job of

---

FAST FACT

Note the difference in the phrasing between these two possible questions; the second is an actual Gallup Poll question.

Would you favor or oppose a national law requiring a seven-day waiting period before a handgun could be purchased?

Would you favor or oppose a national law requiring a seven-day waiting period before a handgun could be purchased, in order to determine whether the prospective buyer has been convicted of a felony or is mentally ill?

forecasting elections and are accurate when measuring public opinion on other issues. However, Americans have a hard time believing that a randomly selected survey of 2,000 people—actually a far larger-than-average sample size for most national polls—could represent the attitudes, opinions, or projected behavior of hundreds of millions of Americans. "Sampling errors" occur when the group being surveyed is not representative—for example, if a poll asked

INTERVIEWER: PLEASE RECORD FOR TABULATION PURPOSES

1a. How long have you lived in this state?.......................
   (Get answer in weeks, months or years)

   □ Always lived here

 b. Have you ever voted in this state?

   □ Yes   □ No

 c. How long have you lived in the COUNTY where you now live?

   ....   □ Always lived here
   (Get answer in weeks, months or years)

2a. Are you interested in the coming election for President?

   □ Yes   □ No

 b. Do you vote in all elections, or only those that interest you?

   □ All   □ Those that interest

   □ Qualified ....

3a. Do you remember FOR CERTAIN whether or not you voted in the 1940 Presidential election?

   [1]□ Yes, voted   [2]□ No, didn't vote
   [3]□ No, too young to vote   [V]□ Don't remember

If YES, VOTED, ask:

 b. Did you vote for Willkie, Roosevelt or Thomas?

   [4]□ Willkie   [5]□ Roosevelt   [6]□ Thomas   [7]□ Other

4. In what country was your father born?.......................

   ....

5a. Is there a telephone in your home?   □ Yes   □ No
If YES, ask:

 b. Is the telephone listed either under your name or the name of a member of your immediate family?   □ Yes   □ No

Classify respondent as: Check whether:
□ W   □ AV   □ OAA   □ Man   □ Wh
□ AV+   □ P   □ OR   □ Woman   □ Cl

Specific occupation ....
   (If housewife or student, record occupation of head of family. If retired or unemployed, record former occupation)

Respondent's age ....

   Please do NOT interview any member of the armed forces.

                                             Form 329_Sc.

A 1944 copy of a Gallup Poll questionnaire on the 1940 presidential election. Polling has become one of the leading ways politicians and lawmakers measure public opinion, but results must be measured against the flaws inherent in the polling system.

Polling results on gun control often change dramatically after school shootings and other highly publicized violent incidents. Former Michigan state representative Laura Baird explains to a reporter in 1999 how she and other Democrats use opinion polls on firearms to introduce and push through gun control legislation.

about the opinions of men only, or of Texas residents, or of college graduates, and then claimed that the results represented the beliefs of all Americans. Almost all polls are open to attack on the grounds that the sample is not representative of the United States, although some polls are clearly more at fault than others.

There are other possible sources of error in polls or surveys that are as serious as sampling errors. Some people—even whole groups of people—refuse to be interviewed. (Depending on the line of questioning, such groups could include drug abusers or those who cheat on their taxes.) The interviewer may be biased or work for an organization that is biased. In addition, it is impossible to be sure of how honest and candid poll respondents are. After all, their "self-reporting" cannot be checked or verified. Some participants in polls give answers that they think will make them look heroic or will bolster their own self-image. Because this self-reported data is never checked, many polls on gun ownership and usage may be little more than a collection of people's fantasies about their own lives and actions.

The wording of a question can also distort a poll. Writing a clear and neutral question on a controversial issue is extremely difficult, and pollsters have an almost limitless range of wording options. In a question asking whether the public favors or opposes legislation regarding guns, should the words *freedom* or *murder* appear? Should the Second Amendment be identified as guaranteeing the "right to bear arms" or the "importance of militias"? When expressing support for a ban on assault weapons, does the public have a clear understanding of the definition of *assault weapon*? Any of these wording choices can have a huge effect on the levels of support recorded in the poll.

Nor do polls accurately measure the intensity of support—that is, how deeply respondents hold their views. A response to a survey is often given on the spur of the moment to a stranger who calls or appears uninvited and asks questions on topics that the respondent knows little about and has given little thought to. Americans are notorious for having opinions on every topic, regardless of whether they know what they're talking about; although this habit makes for entertaining news, it may not reflect whether they actually care about an issue.

With all their flaws, however, polls do play an important role in American life by allowing elected officials to glimpse the public's views. Questions about firearms and gun control have been asked fairly regularly since at least 1970. A single poll cannot possibly be used to understand American popular opinion, but the analysis of polls over a series of years offers one way to construct a snapshot of American beliefs about guns and gun use in the United States.

FAST FACT

Survey respondents can't always be trusted. In a 1994 phone survey of 1,500 adults living in the United States, 6 percent of the respondents reported having had personal contact with aliens from another planet. If this poll were accurate, then 17 million Americans would have experienced extraterrestrial contact.

General Support for Gun Control Measures

In general, support for stricter regulation of firearms has been fairly consistent over the last several decades and may even be growing. Of course, it is possible that the polls that show that Americans support gun control use biased wording or are otherwise seriously flawed; most gun control opponents take this position, based on the failure of this supposed support to produce any meaningful legislation affecting guns. Support for gun control measures also tends to fluctuate based upon the latest criminal gun violence. Significant changes in support occurred after the assassination of President John F. Kennedy in 1963 and popular singer John Lennon in 1980 and the attempted assassination of President Ronald Reagan in 1981.

A photograph of musician John Lennon, killed by a mentally ill fan using a handgun, is displayed in his memory in 1980. Violence against beloved public figures often brings about significant increases in gun control support as more people call for tighter restrictions on firearms.

YEAR	PERCENT IN FAVOR OF GUN PURCHASE PERMITS	PERCENT IN FAVOR OF FEDERAL HANDGUN REGISTRATION
1959	75 percent	N/A
1963	79 percent	N/A
1967	72 percent	N/A
1971	72 percent	N/A
1975	74 percent	77 percent
1980	69 percent	67 percent
1982	72 percent	66 percent
1985	72 percent	70 percent
1990	68 percent	73 percent

What is perhaps most astonishing is the long-term general support for gun control measures. In survey after survey, year after year, respondents strongly supported attempts to limit gun ownership. Over thirty years, support for gun purchase permits and federal handgun registration consistently fell between 66 percent and 80 percent. In any given year, regardless of immediate news, no less than three out of every five Americans favored moderate gun control measures.

Clear majorities of Americans also favored firearms regulations such as waiting periods, owner licenses, and concealed-carry permits. Equally consistent, on the other hand, is the opposition in polls to a complete ban on handguns in this period. At no time in any poll between 1960 and 1990 did such a ban receive majority support, although the proposal usually receives the endorsement of about one out of three Americans.

In a 1990 survey commissioned by *Time* magazine, 87 percent of all gun owners interviewed favored a federal law requiring a seven-day waiting period and background check for anyone wanting to purchase a handgun. At least

FAST FACT

In 1998, a Harris poll claimed that the proportion of all adults who reported that they had a gun of any kind in their homes fell to 32 percent, compared to 48 percent in 1973 and 40 percent in 1996. This sharp drop in two years seems extreme and almost certainly reflected an unwillingness to admit to owning a gun after several well-publicized incidents in the 1990s of children obtaining guns in their home or someone else's home and using them to murder classmates.

YEAR	PERCENT IN FAVOR OF A BAN ON HANDGUN POSSESSION
1975	37 percent
1978	31 percent
1981	39 percent
1987	42 percent
1990	36 percent

half of those respondents also favored mandatory registration of rifles, shotguns, handguns, and semiautomatic weapons.

Polls and School Shootings

The 1990s were marked by a series of notorious incidents in which students killed their classmates, often with high-powered firearms. These sensational school shootings generated numerous polls about the role of guns in American life. Surveys in the 1990s showed that the American public—including gun owners—continued to favor gun regulation by large margins, often two or three to one. However, support for gun control measures did not noticeably increase in the decade, despite the widespread publicity about youngsters being murdered with firearms.

For example, a nationwide Harris poll in April 1998 found that two-thirds of all adults supported "stricter gun control," while only 23 percent favored "less strict gun control." Among gun owners, a smaller majority, 57 percent, preferred more regulation. Of the general sample, 76 percent supported stricter control of handguns, while 66 percent of gun owners claimed they would support such a measure.

In April 1999, after the massacre at Columbine High School in Littleton, Colorado, President Bill Clinton, joined by many Democrats in Congress, pressed for renewed gun control measures. However, in August 1999, an ABC News poll revealed that although 63 percent of

Americans favored stricter gun control laws, support was no higher than it had been in ABC polls for the entire decade: 64 percent in October 1993 and 60 percent in June 1989. The number peaked at 67 percent in May 1999, a month after the Columbine High School shootings.

Nevertheless, there was an apparently greater intensity in gun control support in the 1990s. In 1989, only 28 percent "strongly" backed tougher gun control, according to ABC polling, whereas ten years later, 46 percent reported that they took that position. This was twice as many as those who "strongly" opposed it. All age, income, race, and education groups favored tougher gun laws, but support remained noticeably higher among women (73 percent) than men (51 percent). This female support for greater restrictions on gun ownership was reflected in a "Million Mom March" on Mother's Day (May 14), 2000. Hundreds of thousands of mothers (and others) gathered in Washington, D.C., and elsewhere to call on lawmakers to pass stricter gun control laws.

A still image from the videotape taken of the Columbine High School cafeteria in Littleton, Colorado, shows Eric Harris (left), and Dylan Klebold, who carries a semiautomatic pistol. Surprisingly, public support for gun control did not increase by any significant amount in the wake of this well-publicized violence.

The international community is experiencing the effects of lax gun control legislation as well. In 2003, a sixteen-year-old boy killed himself after firing at his teacher in a classroom in Coburg, Germany. In this photograph, a policeman looks on as the boy's coffin is transported.

In 2000, a Harris poll found that a 63 percent majority favored stricter gun control, and an even larger 72 percent majority favored stricter control of handguns. These numbers also had not changed a great deal since June 1999, despite the enormous media coverage of school shootings and gun violence and the public debate about trigger locks, gun sales, and other gun safety issues. A Gallup/CNN/*USA Today* survey taken in June 1999—only two months after the Littleton massacre—showed that the number of Americans who favored stricter gun laws had declined by 20 percent since 1990. An Associated Press (AP) poll released on the one-year anniversary of the Littleton shootings indicated that Americans favored strict enforcement of existing laws over new gun laws by 42 to 33 percent. These results were seconded by a Gallup poll in September 2000, which showed that 53 percent of Americans wanted stricter enforcement of existing firearms laws but no new laws, while 45 percent wanted both stricter enforcement of current gun laws and new gun control laws.

So although support for greater gun regulations remained high after the Columbine massacre, it did not grow appreciably. As a result, Congress passed almost no new gun control measures. Some of the suggested legislation that did not pass included closing the "gun show loophole" (referring to the ability of private sellers to avoid following federal law regarding gun sales); requiring mandatory trigger locks on all new handguns; raising the age for buying guns from eighteen to twenty-one; and banning the import of high-capacity ammunition clips. An occasional school shooting—and even the sniper in Washington, D.C., who killed ten people in 2002 with an illegally owned rifle designed specifically to get around the assault weapons ban of 1994—did not lead to any huge popular movement for gun control laws.

The New Millennium

Despite the supposed support for gun control in the polls, Americans expressed very little criticism of Congress over the lack of gun legislation after the Columbine High School shootings. In 2001, 41 percent expressed vague, general dissatisfaction with the way that Congress handled the issue of guns in America, but only 18 percent claimed to be angry with Congress for its refusal to regulate firearms.

In the first few years of the twenty-first century, support for increased regulation of firearms remained closely tied to the belief that this policy would be effective in reducing crime. An ABC News poll in early 2001 noted that interest in gun control was highest among Americans who believed that the regulation of firearms would decrease violence. Among those who thought that it would reduce crime "a lot," 87 percent stated that it was "very important" to pass new gun control legislation. Among those who thought that it would reduce violence "somewhat," 75 percent called it "very important."

However, for those who didn't think that it would reduce violent crime at all—48 percent of the survey—only 27 percent called it "very important" for Congress to act. This means that nearly half of the American public thought that gun control would not do anything at all to reduce violent crime in this country. Along the same lines, a survey by the Pew Research Center in April 2000 indicated that only 6 percent of Americans believed that tougher gun laws would help to prevent future school shootings.

The contested presidential election of 2000, the controversial tax cuts advocated by President George W. Bush after he took office, and the terrorist attacks on the United States in 2001 all operated to remove gun violence as a crucial national issue. President Bush set the tone by emphasizing the responsibility of the individual rather than the weapon in criminal behavior; after one high school shooting in 2001, Bush simply stated, "All of us must be mindful that some people may decide to act out their own aggressions."

In the years following the 2000 election, stricter gun regulation not only was dead, but the trend was in the other direction—to loosen gun regulations in the United States. In 2003, the U.S. House of Representatives passed the so-called Protection of Legal Commerce in Arms Act, by a 285 to 140 vote (221 to 3 among Republicans). This legislation states that no one can bring a lawsuit in any state or federal court against a manufacturer or seller of firearms if the case is based on the unlawful acts of people who misuse guns. Polls seemed to indicate widespread public support.

What Gun Laws Will Americans Support?

In 2001, 63 percent of Americans favored stricter gun control laws—approximately the same percentage of support in every year since 1990. "Strong" support, however, continued to increase, especially for some specific proposals such as mandatory safety locks and background checks at gun shows. In 2003, the public split evenly on a ban against carrying concealed weapons. A third of Americans continued to support an outright ban on the sale of handguns.

When the ABC News poll of 2001 asked respondents whether they would support certain policies, these were the levels of support.

Background checks at gun shows	90 percent
Mandatory trigger locks	79 percent
Ban on assault weapons	77 percent
Registration of handgun owners	75 percent
Ban on mail-order and Internet gun sales	66 percent
Ban on carrying a concealed weapon	49 percent
Ban on handgun sales except to police	32 percent

Pro-gun demonstrators rally outside the statehouse in Boston in 2000 to demand that lawmakers loosen some of the restrictions mandated by the state's new, tough gun control laws.

Gender Gap

Support for gun control differed by population group; people who don't own guns, self-declared Democrats, and women were most likely to support restrictions on gun use. The so-called Million Mom March of 2000 seemed to reveal what polls had indicated for a long time: There was a serious difference in opinion between men and women over gun control.

Gun use, whether for hunting, self-defense, or crime, is closely associated in the popular mind with men and masculinity. The 1990s were notable for a vast expansion of the American prison population. In 1980, only about

Donna Dees-Thomases, the mother who initiated the idea of the Million Mom March, a rally to support gun control, holds up a poster promoting the event in 2000. The march raised public awareness of the importance of gun control legislation.

500,000 Americans were behind bars; this number rose to 1.1 million in 1990 and more than 2.1 million people in 2002. More Americans are in jail than in any other nation in the world—and the large majority of these are men. The most horrific and widely publicized acts of violence, such as school shootings, sniper incidents, and membership in militia organizations, involved men and boys. Popular stereotypes identified a pro-gun vote as "masculine" and a gun control vote as comparatively feminine, or at least less masculine. According to a 2001 poll, women were far less likely than men to own guns and considerably more likely to support measures restricting and/or regulating gun ownership.

Some women, however, supported gun ownership and fewer restrictions on firearms. Gun manufacturers in particular encouraged women shooters as a way to expand the industry into a vast, untapped market. The National Rifle Association (NRA) elected two women as representative spokespeople in the 1990s and actively promoted its "Refuse to Be a Victim" program. This program recommended that women acquire handguns for use in self-defense and asserted that gun ownership was a triumph for feminist values. The NRA also joined with several firearms manufacturers and hunting organizations to support the "Becoming an Outdoors-Woman" program, which ran in more than thirty-five states. In

POLICY	PERCENT SUPPORT AMONG	
	MEN	WOMEN
Stricter gun control	51 percent	73 percent
Background checks at gun shows	84 percent	95 percent
Mandatory trigger locks	67 percent	89 percent
Ban on assault weapons	67 percent	86 percent
Registration of handgun owners	66 percent	84 percent
Ban on mail-order and Internet gun sales	62 percent	69 percent
Ban on carrying a concealed weapon	44 percent	55 percent
Ban on handgun sales except to police	25 percent	39 percent

states where legislation was being debated that would allow the right to carry concealed handguns, women often came forward as pro-gun supporters and received a great deal of publicity. Organizations such as Women Against Gun Control suggested using women's economic power to boycott major American companies that "have proven themselves to be enemies of the Second Amendment." In 1993, the National Shooting Sports Foundation (NSSF) organized a Women's Shooting Sports Foundation.

Even women who use guns, however, sometimes faced a backlash from their male counterparts. In the 1992 Olympic Games, Zhang Shan, a Chinese skeet shooter, became the first woman to earn a gold medal in a mixed shooting event. She won the traditionally male-dominated shotgun event by beating the field of forty men and five women. Male shooters were apparently so threatened by Shan's success that the International Shooting Union changed the format for the 1996 Olympics, requiring men and women to compete separately.

Limits of Popular Opinion

The obvious question raised by these hundreds of surveys is why the public support for gun control over the last twenty years has not produced any meaningful regulation. Large majorities of Americans claim to support mandatory national handgun registration, mandatory trigger locks, background checks at gun shows, and other gun control measures. The number of Americans who say they "strongly" support gun control rose from 28 percent in 1989 to 52 percent in 2000. Nonetheless, there is relatively low public pressure for gun control legislation. Even high-profile shootings like those at Columbine High School in 1999 or the Washington, D.C., sniper murders of 2002 did not lead to a groundswell of support for greater control of firearms.

It is possible, of course, that the polls have been incorrect or consistently biased over the last thirty years.

This is the position of one lawyer who opposed gun control restrictions. He claimed,

> Among the greatest assets of the American gun prohibition movement are certain professional pollsters. While citizen mail to elected officials is overwhelmingly pro-rights, pollsters often do an excellent job of convincing elected officials that "the public" favors repressive gun control. But in truth, many polls are little more than thinly disguised propaganda for the anti-gun lobby.

On the other hand, supporters of gun control claim that the support is real enough, but laws cannot be passed because of the power and influence of advocacy groups such as the NRA.

In general, however, gun control is not a determining issue for most voters; many people do not think or care much about it or have stable opinions one way or another. Gun control scored quite low in a list of voting issues for

The proliferation of the Internet has significantly increased illegal sales and purchases of firearms. In 1999, New York senator Charles Schumer showed reporters an enlargement of a computer screen displaying a Web site where guns may be purchased.

the 2000 presidential election. When respondents were asked the relative importance of fifteen items in making their decision on Election Day, the candidate's position on gun control ranked a modest twelfth out of the fifteen. When asked to rank the issues that Congress should handle in 2000, 55 percent of those polled called it very important to enact tougher gun control measures, but this compared to about 80 percent for laws protecting patients' rights, Social Security, and Medicare. Support for gun control in the United States appears to be very wide but not particularly deep, often amounting to little more than an answer to a poll question.

CHAPTER 2

Politics and Lobbying

Gun control is sometimes seen as one of the basic cultural issues that divides the two major political parties in the United States. The national Democratic and Republican Parties usually try to win voters in the center of American politics and often avoid any meaningful disagreement with each other, yet they have consistently disagreed over the value of gun control. With large exceptions, the Democratic Party has generally backed gun regulation, while the Republican Party has supported individual gun ownership free of government control. Although tougher gun control laws received majority support in all age, income, race, and education groups in a 2001 poll, self-identified Republicans were less likely to favor tougher gun laws (52 percent) compared to Democrats (81 percent).

In poll after poll for more than thirty years, large majorities of Americans consistently claim to favor stricter gun control laws. Support goes even higher for a range of specific proposals, such as mandatory trigger locks and background checks at gun shows. About a third of Americans see nothing wrong with an outright ban on the sale of handguns. However, the popular desire to regulate gun ownership and usage rarely is transformed into law, and usually only after enormous controversy. Opponents of gun regulations believe that the polls are biased or inaccurate, misrepresenting the people's actual intent. They feel that Americans' true beliefs are reflected in the lack of concern over the absence of firearms legislation. On the other hand, supporters of increased restrictions on gun ownership and usage believe that the polls are accurate, but that advocacy groups such as the National Rifle Association (NRA) thwart the will of the people.

Democrats and Republicans

The official platforms of the Democratic and Republican Parties, written and publicized every presidential election year, provide a rough idea of the positions of the two major parties. Before 1968, the question of firearms control was not a major issue in American national party politics. The gun issue first appeared in party platforms in 1968, reflecting the passage of the Gun Control Act of 1968 and the assassinations of civil rights leader Martin Luther King Jr. and New York senator Robert Kennedy. Both parties initially agreed that firearms possession was out of control. The Democratic Party pledged to "promote the passage and enforcement of effective federal, state and local gun control legislation," while the Republican platform promised "enactment of legislation to control indiscriminate availability of firearms."

By 1972, President Richard Nixon's "southern strategy" set the Republican Party on the ultimately successful path to win over the voters of the southern states. These voters had traditionally voted Democratic, but many of them were unhappy with the national Democratic Party's support of civil rights legislation. Because the South (along with parts of the West) was the

In 1980, gun owners supporting the Republican Party helped Ronald Reagan beat incumbent Democrat Jimmy Carter for the United States presidency. The Republican platform has, over time, sought to loosen restrictions in gun control legislation.

area of the United States with the highest percentage of gun owners, opposition to firearms regulation was a natural fit for the new Republican strategy.

The 1972 Republican Party platform continued to pledge that Republicans would "intensify efforts to prevent criminal access to all weapons, including special emphasis on cheap, readily-obtainable handguns." However, the platform also emphasized "the right of responsible citizens to collect, own and use firearms for legitimate purposes, including hunting, target shooting and self-defense."

Election by election, the Republican Party shifted away from any support of firearms regulation, replacing it with calls in the party platform for stricter enforcement of criminal statutes already on the books such as "automatic and mandatory minimum sentences for criminals." The party platforms in 1980, 1984, and 1988 stated that Republicans defended the "constitutional right to keep and bear arms" (without any mention of militias). In 1980, that wording included an added phrase urging removal of

Actor Charlton Heston, past president of the powerful gun lobby, the National Rifle Association, lent a famous Republican face to the proceedings at the Republican National Convention in Dallas, Texas, in 1984.

"those provisions of the Gun Control Act of 1968 that do not significantly impact on crime but serve rather to restrain the law-abiding citizen in his legitimate use of firearms." When Ronald Reagan was elected president in 1980, the ideas in this sentence were put into action in the Firearms Owners' Protection Act, which was passed with considerable Democratic support. By 1992, the Republican Party platform declared that support for gun control was not merely a difference of opinion but actively treasonous because it was harmful to national security: "We note that those who seek to disarm citizens in their homes are the same liberals who tried to disarm our Nation during the Cold War and are today seeking to cut our national defense below safe levels."

At the same time, the Democratic Party took firmer stands on gun control, which served to solidify the party's advantage in most urban areas. The 1972 platform declared, "There must be laws to control the improper use of handguns. Effective legislation must include a ban on sale of handguns known as Saturday night specials which are unsuitable for sporting purposes." The 1980 platform defensively affirmed "the right of sportsmen to possess guns for purely hunting and target-shooting purposes. However, handguns simplify and intensify violent crimes." Democratic Party platforms from 1984 to 1996 basically supported gun control measures such as waiting periods and "assault weapons controls." This position was consistent with the Democratic Party's general belief in governmental regulation on the national level for the public good.

The Party Platforms of 2000

Immediately after the bloody Columbine school shootings in 1999, Vice President Al Gore went to Colorado to offer soothing words and support for tougher firearms laws. "It is too easy for a young child to get a gun, and everywhere we look, there are too many lessons in how to use one," Gore said. "We can do something about that." Even

Republican presidential candidate George W. Bush said after Columbine that "we ought to keep guns out of the hands of children like those," although he quickly added that the government can't make people love each other. The Democratic Party, sensing a campaign issue in 2000, pushed for stricter laws making parents liable for gun crimes committed by their children and tried to pass national legislation requiring mandatory safety locks and toughening restrictions on sales at gun shows. Those proposals died in Congress, although gun control advocates did have some state successes.

Basic philosophical differences between the Democratic and Republican Parties over gun control were apparent in the presidential election of 2000. The Democratic Party nominated Vice President Al Gore from Tennessee and boasted of his role in passing the gun control measure known as the Brady Handgun Violence Protection Act of 1993 (or the Brady Bill). The party's official platform stated,

> Bill Clinton and Al Gore...stood up to the gun lobby to pass the Brady Bill and ban deadly assault weapons and stopped nearly half a million felons, fugitives, and stalkers from buying guns...serious crime is down seven years in a row, to its lowest level in a quarter-century. Violent crime is down by 24 percent. The number of juveniles committing homicides with guns is down nearly 60 percent.... We can't surrender to the right-wing Republicans who threatened funding for new police, who tried to gut crime prevention, and who would invite the NRA into the Oval Office.... The Columbine tragedy struck America's heart, but in its wake Republicans have done nothing to keep guns away from those who shouldn't have them.... Now we must do even more.... We need mandatory child safety locks, to protect our children. We should require a photo license I.D., a full background check, and a gun safety test to buy a new handgun in America.

On the other hand, the Republican Party nominated Texas governor George W. Bush, who had so passionately supported pro-gun positions and legislation in Texas that one leader of the NRA said that the organization would be working out of the White House in a Bush administration. Vice presidential candidate Dick Cheney, when representing Wyoming in the House of Representatives in the 1980s, had voted against a ban on armor-piercing bullets (so-called cop-killer bullets) and against regulating plastic handguns that might evade detection by airport metal detectors. The Republican Party platform stated,

While campaigning for the U.S. Senate in 1999, Republican candidate Jim Miller (center) talked to vendors at a gun show in Bealton, Virginia. Many Republicans have the support of people in the gun industry because of the party's favorable voting records on looser gun restrictions.

> We defend the constitutional right to keep and
> bear arms, and we affirm the individual
> responsibility to safely use and store firearms.
> Because self-defense is a basic human right, we will
> promote training in their safe storage, especially in
> federal programs for women and the elderly....
> Although we support background checks to ensure

that guns do not fall into the hands of criminals, we oppose federal licensing of law-abiding gun owners, and national registration as a violation of the Second Amendment and an invasion of privacy of honest citizens.... We will hold criminals individually accountable for their actions by strong enforcement of federal and state firearm laws, especially when guns are used in violent or drug-related crimes.

President Bill Clinton defended himself against attacks by the National Rifle Association throughout his presidency. In 2000, he was joined by a bipartisan congressional delegation calling for legislators to resume gun safety talks on Capitol Hill. New York representative Carolyn McCarthy (at the lectern), whose husband was killed by gun violence, described how the NRA pressures members of Congress to avoid voting on gun control motions.

The Election of 2000

A poll in May 2000 found that a 63 percent majority of Americans favored stricter gun control, and an even larger 72 percent majority favored closer control of handguns. However, this support did not seem to greatly benefit Vice President Al Gore or the Democrats. In the eighteen

months between the Columbine murders and the presidential election, Democratic efforts to increase firearms regulation had failed even with a pro-gun-control Democratic president in the White House.

Democrats' hopes to make gun control a big issue in the 2000 campaign may actually have backfired and cost Al Gore the election. The presidential election of 2000 was one of the closest in American history. Only by winning the disputed votes in the state of Florida did Bush defeat Gore for the presidency. In losing the election, Gore narrowly lost the key (and often Democratic) states of West Virginia, Arkansas (Democratic president Bill Clinton's home state), and Tennessee (Gore's own home state). Some analysts believed that Gore's support of gun control caused him to lose these crucial swing states, where gun ownership was high, hunting was an important recreational pastime, and gun advocates were a crucial single-issue voting bloc. At the same time, Gore's support of gun control apparently did not help him win any key states where his margins were greater and other issues were more relevant. Exit polls in the 2000 election revealed that about half of voters had a gun in their household and half did not. Of those who came from gun-owning homes, Bush won 61 percent to 36 percent. Among nongun owners, Al Gore prevailed, 58 percent to 39 percent.

In addition, many candidates who were backed by gun control supporters lost their positions in 2000, and most of those endorsed by the NRA were victorious. The Republican control of Congress meant that the possibility of increased gun control legislation on a national level was extremely poor. Ironically, one of the gun control supporters' few victories—the defeat of Republican John Ashcroft by Jean Carnahan for senator of Missouri—backfired, because Ashcroft went on to become attorney general in the Bush administration and tilt the Justice Department to a pro-gun position. However, Oregon and Colorado voters did approve a requirement for background checks for buyers at gun shows, overturning previous defeats on the legislative level.

The Muting of the Political Gun Control Debate

According to a 2001 poll, majorities of Americans, regardless of their party affiliation, continued to support a wide range of gun control legislation. However, people who declared themselves to be Democrats were far more likely to support gun control legislation than Republicans.

Nonetheless, after the terrorist attacks in 2001, Democrats became reluctant to take an anti-gun position. They apparently feared that such a stance would be equated in the popular mind with being "soft" on defense and terrorism. Democrats, who pushed hard for new firearms regulations after the Columbine High School massacre in 1999, were also resigned to the fact that a pro-gun president and Republican control of Congress meant little prospect of the passage of stricter gun regulations.

For example, on the same day in July 2003, five factory workers in Mississippi were shot to death by a coworker, and five people in a family in Bakersfield, California, were killed with gunfire, yet there were almost no angry speeches in Congress or new proposals to crack down on firearms. Instead, the official Republican Party position was that gun violence was a problem that should be combated by punishing and deterring gun criminals, not by federal regulation of ownership of firearms. President

LEGISLATION	PERCENT SUPPORT AMONG	
	DEMOCRATS	REPUBLICANS
Stricter gun control	73 percent	49 percent
Background checks at gun shows	95 percent	90 percent
Mandatory trigger locks	86 percent	76 percent
Ban on assault weapons	84 percent	72 percent
Ban on mail-order and Internet gun sales	67 percent	62 percent
Registration of handgun owners	84 percent	65 percent
Ban on carrying a concealed weapon	56 percent	39 percent
Ban on handgun sales except to police	39 percent	27 percent

George W. Bush called a school shooting in San Diego in 2001 a "disgraceful act of cowardice," but implied that the solution had nothing to do with politics or the government: "All adults in society can teach children right from wrong, can explain that life is precious," he told reporters.

Twelve-year-old Doris Payne (left), and Allyson Webb mourn the deaths of five Lockheed plant workers in Meridian, Mississippi, in 2003. The shooting of the employees by an "angry" coworker brandishing a shotgun and a rifle was all but ignored by Republican policy makers in Congress.

Anti-Gun-Control Measures

The Republican Party, in control of the presidency in 2000 and controlling both houses of Congress after 2002, moved to roll back gun regulations and protect gun manufacturers and dealers. House majority leader Tom DeLay, a Republican from Texas, claimed in 2003 that there would not be enough votes in the House of Representatives to renew Congress's 1994 ban on certain types of so-called assault weapons when that law expired in 2004. In another case, Republican senator Orrin Hatch of Utah, the chair of the Senate Judiciary Committee, introduced a bill to repeal the extremely tough gun control laws that had been passed in Washington, D.C., in 1976 (the district is partially run by Congress). He said,

> All too often, we read in the paper about yet another vicious murder carried out against an innocent District of Columbia resident. Try to imagine the horror that the victim felt when he faced a gun-toting criminal and could not legally reach for a firearm to protect himself. We must act now to stop the carnage and put law-abiding citizens in a position to exercise their right to self-defense.

In 2001, President George W. Bush's new attorney general, John Ashcroft, outlined a new and controversial position of the U.S. government, which reversed the Justice Department's traditional interpretation of the Second Amendment. Ashcroft claimed that the U.S. government now believed that the Second Amendment "protects the gun ownership rights of individuals,

In 2003, in Cincinnati, Ohio, anti-gun protester Aaron Rodgers marches alongside citizens calling for legislation to allow ordinary people to carry concealed weapons.

including persons who are not members of the militia to bear firearms."

In October 2001, the Fifth U.S. Circuit Court of Appeals in New Orleans, Louisiana, supported by the U.S. government, ruled in *United States v. Emerson* that it agreed with this individualist interpretation of the Second Amendment. The shift in government policy led immediately to several legal challenges to American gun laws. However, in January 2004, a federal judge appointed by President Bush rejected a lawsuit challenging Washington's ban on the sale and possession of handguns on Second Amendment grounds. In *Seegars v. Ashcroft*, the judge ruled that the "Court must conclude that the Second Amendment does not confer an individual right to possess firearms. Rather, the Amendment's objective is to ensure the vitality of state militias."

In 2003, Congress attempted to pass a bill that would prevent victims of gun crimes from bringing civil lawsuits against firearms manufacturers and dealers. This bill was modeled after similar laws passed by state legislatures that created legal immunity from liability exclusively for the gun industry; as governor of Texas, George W. Bush had supported and signed one of these laws. In April 2003, while most of the nation's attention was focused on Iraq, the U.S. House of Representatives passed HR 1036, the so-called Protection of Legal Commerce in Arms Act, by a 285 to 140 vote. The vote was an astonishing 221 to 3 among Republican legislators, and they were joined by sixty-three Democrats.

HR 1036 states that no one can bring a lawsuit in any state or federal court against a manufacturer or seller of firearms if the case is based upon the unlawful acts of people who misuse guns. The bill specifies certain types of lawsuits that would still be allowable, including those against a person who transfers a gun knowing that it will be used to commit a violent crime, or actions for damages resulting directly from a defect in design or manufacture of a firearm.

Supporters of legal immunity argue that the gun industry needs special protection in order to prevent people from blaming manufacturers and dealers when a criminal misuses a gun. A lawyer for the NSSF stated that "if a dealer sells a legal product to a consumer who has undergone a criminal background check and filled out the federally required forms, and [who] later gives that gun to someone else to commit a crime, that dealer should not be sued." S 659, a similar bill, was debated in the U.S. Senate in the fall of 2003, where it was supported by several top Democrats. Senate minority whip Harry Reid, a Democrat from Nevada, was a cosponsor, and Senate minority leader Tom Daschle from South Dakota also offered support. Final action on the bill is still pending.

Gun Control: Not a Strictly Partisan Issue

The two-to-one voting margin on HR 1036 in the House of Representatives indicates that despite the disagreement of the political parties, gun control is far from a party-line issue. Republican administrations have often been associated with gun control legislation. It was President George H.W. Bush who banned the import of assault weapons in 1989 and promoted the view that Americans should be allowed to own only weapons suitable for "sporting purposes." In 1991, ex-president Ronald Reagan stated, "I support [the passage of] the Brady Bill...and I urge the Congress to enact it without further delay." Rudolph Giuliani, the former Republican mayor of New York City, took strongly pro-gun-control stands; his administration sued twenty-six gun manufacturers in June 2000 and proposed a nationwide plan for gun licensing, complete with yearly safety inspections. Another Republican, New York State governor George Pataki, signed into law one of the nation's strictest gun control programs in 2000.

On the Democratic side, Representative John Dingell from Michigan is a staunch foe of all gun regulations and a former board member of the NRA. The NRA often endorses Democratic candidates, such as Vermont governor Howard Dean, who was a presidential contender in 2004.

A CBS poll in November 2003 revealed a link between party affiliation and support for gun control, but stricter firearms regulation continued to receive support across the political spectrum. The poll asked, "In general, do you think gun control laws should be made more strict, less strict, or kept as they are now?" Republicans endorsed stricter laws by a 40 percent to 14 percent margin for keeping the laws as they were. Independents backed them by a 48 percent to 12 percent margin and Democrats supported stricter gun laws by a margin of 65 percent to 4 percent.

Gun use and attitudes toward guns sometimes differ as much from region to region and state to state as they do between the political parties. A breakdown of many gun control votes reveals that area of residence is more of a predictor than whether the elected official is a Democrat

FAST FACT

The southern United States has higher homicide rates, especially those involving guns, than any other region.

Local gun control advocacy groups often take the issue to the grassroots level. In Philadelphia, Pennsylvania, in 1999, the Philadelphia Anti-Drug/Anti-Violence Network announces its seventh annual Gun Turn In. Reverend Efrain Cotto, a local pastor, delivers a prayer during the press conference kicking off the event.

John Kinkade, manager of a sporting goods store in Des Moines, Iowa, holds one of the rifles for sale. In addition to federal law requiring gun dealers to do a background check with the FBI system, Iowa law also requires local background checks for handguns.

or Republican. In general, in areas where hunting is popular and gun ownership is widespread, there is less support for policies to regulate firearms. The strongest opposition to gun regulations comes from southern, western, and rural representatives, regardless of party, while the greatest support usually arises from urban politicians, especially in the Northeast.

Therefore, the political debate over gun use in the United States has a geographical element based on gun ownership. One poll in the 1990s concluded that gun ownership ranged from a low of 29 percent in New England to a high of 60 percent in the central southeast region (for example, Arkansas and Tennessee). While quite large, this regional gap is smaller than in previous years; in the 1970s, gun ownership ran from 24 percent in New England to 72 percent in the central southeast region. About 13 percent of New England and mid-Atlantic state residents ever purchased a gun, compared to 26 to 30 percent in five southern and western regions. New Jersey, New York, and Massachusetts had the lowest gun

ownership levels (16 to 22 percent), while Tennessee and North Carolina had the highest (55 to 59 percent).

Background Check Law

An example of how the Democrats and Republicans can occasionally work together on firearms issues took place in 2003, when Congress passed a bill that would provide more than $1 billion to prevent felons, illegal immigrants, and others from buying guns. Gun groups had complained that it took too long for many purchases to be approved by the FBI, mainly because its system was overloaded from conducting background checks on 7 million prospective gun buyers each year. Gun control groups also criticized the system, asserting that thousands of felons, spouse abusers, and people with histories of mental illness continued to be able to buy guns.

The new legislation provided state agencies and courts with more than $300 million a year through 2006 to upgrade their databases on criminals and others banned by federal law from buying guns. States that did not meet certain performance standards were penalized by losing federal grant money. The bill was supported both by longtime gun advocates Larry Craig (Republican senator from Idaho) and John Dingell, as well as staunch gun control supporters like Charles Schumer (Democratic senator from New York) and Carolyn McCarthy (Democratic representative from New York).

Intensity of Views

If polls consistently imply that Americans favor more restrictive firearms regulation, why doesn't that impulse translate into political gains for gun control advocates? Despite several high-profile school shootings and sniper incidents, Americans do not seem to be outraged over the failure of Congress to pass legislation.

There are several possible reasons for this. Nearly half the public thinks that gun control wouldn't do anything

> **FAST FACT**
>
> U. S. representative Carolyn McCarthy led a quiet life as a nurse and mother until December 7, 1993. On that day, a crazed gunman killed her husband and injured her son in a Long Island Rail Road commuter train. The killer randomly shot passengers with a semiautomatic pistol that was purchased legally in California but not licensed in New York. McCarthy turned the incident into a public campaign against gun violence and was elected to Congress in 1996.

at all to reduce violent crime in the United States, according to an ABC News/*Washington Post* poll in 2000. Although about three out of every ten Americans believe that gun control would reduce violence a great deal, it's relatively low on their priority list, and very few choose a candidate based on the issue.

There's also little personal activism in support of gun control—a crucial element for the success of a single-issue pressure group. Pro-gun-control opinion is generally more weakly held than anti-gun-control opinion and therefore rarely generates sustained legislative action. Gun control opponents, while in the minority in all polls, do a much better job of projecting their voices. In surveys, gun control supporters indicated that they held their views as intensely as those who opposed further restrictions. However, a 2001 poll revealed that gun control opponents were almost twice as likely as gun control supporters to have given money to an organization concerned with the issue (19 percent to 11 percent) and almost twice as likely to have voted for or against a candidate based on his or her position on firearms regulation (19 percent to 11 percent). Gun control opponents were also more likely to have contacted a public official about gun control issues (13 percent to 9 percent).

The most likely explanation for the difference between the poll results and the political results is that people who own firearms make up the majority of opponents to gun regulation in the United States. These gun owners have a personal stake in the passage or rejection of gun control legislation. Many Americans who own, enjoy, or rely on guns—probably about 40 percent of the nation—feel that they might suffer personally if more restrictive gun legislation were passed. On the other hand, supporters of more restrictive regulations for gun ownership rarely have anything personal at stake. Instead, they support gun control on the vague conceptual grounds that it will make the United States safer and improve the nation for everyone. For one gun control opponent, the personal commitment of gun owners explained away the poll results: "Concrete and immediate personal costs motivate behavior more strongly than abstract shared benefits that may or may not materialize sometime in the future."

Lobbying and Politics

In general, supporters of stronger gun regulations do not believe that the polls are incorrect or that their side is less committed. Instead, they claim that gun control opponents are more likely to act on their beliefs only because of the efficiency of gun advocacy groups in mobilizing supporters. They complain that these groups weaken democracy; by lobbying lawmakers and making campaign contributions, they prevent the people's will, as expressed in polls, from being turned into legislation. (To *lobby* is to try to influence lawmakers or public opinion to support or oppose a particular issue or cause.)

Representative Carolyn McCarthy, D-NY (left), accompanied by Nan Aron, president of Alliance for Justice, and Representative Henry Waxman, D-CA, meet reporters on Capitol Hill in December 2001 to denounce efforts by the gun lobby and gun manufacturers to use the events of September 11 to increase gun ownership.

Nonetheless, gun control advocates have tried to form their own lobbying organizations—so far with less impact.

The successes of the civil rights movement in the 1950s and 1960s spurred the growth of single-interest lobbying on topics such as abortion, school prayer, and the death penalty. These groups maintain a narrow and intense focus on one specific issue; members often view the issue in fundamental moral terms—good (their side) and evil (the other side). Single-issue lobbying groups often rely on grassroots activism and winning over public opinion to their side. Supporters see lobbying not as a weakening of democracy, but as a crucial democratic right, the only way that masses of people can actually affect legislation.

The NRA is by far the most influential advocacy group on gun use in the United States. The NRA was founded in 1871 to promote sport shooting, hunting, and firearms

At the National Rifle Association Museum in Fairfax, Virginia, visitors can see displays of guns owned by U.S. presidents, antique guns, and life-sized dioramas illustrating the art and technology of guns. The NRA began as an organization dedicated to hunting and shooting sports, and only in the last few decades has it taken a political stance.

safety. Although the NRA is more than 130 years old, the strong political stance that defines the modern organization dates only from the group's annual meeting in Cincinnati in 1977. In the late 1960s and early 1970s, the NRA had split into two factions: an older remnant, interested in hunting and the shooting sports; and a newer, more ideological group who viewed gun ownership less as a recreational issue than a political one. In what is sometimes called "the Cincinnati Revolt," the more politically inclined members successfully ousted the old leadership and took control of the NRA. "Beginning at this place and at this hour," the new NRA president stated, "this period in the NRA is finished."

Making opposition to any and all gun control a basic principle of the NRA, these hardliners led the organization into a period of remarkable growth. Although many old-timers left the NRA—especially members interested mostly in sport shooting, who were uncomfortable with the new political line—they were more than replaced by newcomers in tune with the new NRA's desire to become "the gun lobby." Membership tripled from 900,000 to nearly 3 million (peaking at about 3.5 million in 1995), and the organization gained its reputation as a nearly invincible gun lobby that would battle absolutely any gun control measure. Between 1968 and 1988, no gun control measure left a congressional committee to be voted on in either the Senate or the House of Representatives.

In the late 1980s and early 1990s, gun control proponents began to press their case for stronger national laws with greater effectiveness and skill. Handgun Control, Inc. (HCI; renamed the Brady Campaign to Prevent Gun Violence in 2001) consciously set out to imitate the lobbying and organizational tactics that worked so well for the NRA. The organization specifically tried to counter the power of the NRA through imitating its success in campaign spending, lobbying, and media. In 2000, however, HCI's resources were still only about one-tenth the size of the NRA's, and its membership barely exceeded 400,000. In 1995, the NRA's annual budget was about $150 million, most of which came from membership dues. That year, the NRA maintained a staff of 300 employees, including more than fifty specifically assigned to lobbying efforts.

After the Oklahoma City terrorist bombing of 1995, the NRA tried to alter its public image from being "anti-gun-control" to "anti-crime." NRA literature states, "Armed criminals aren't just the greatest threat to your life and family. They're also the greatest threat to your Second Amendment right to own a gun. It is their violent misuse of firearms that makes your firearms the target for gun-ban groups, anti-gun politicians and the media."

However, the NRA still took a hard line to preserve gun rights. In October 2003, it was revealed that the NRA had compiled and posted online a controversial, nineteen-page list to allow its members to know which individuals and corporations had anti-gun views or had supported anti-gun causes. The list included actor Kevin Costner, singer Shania Twain, talk-show host Oprah Winfrey, former president Jimmy Carter, and organizations such as the American Jewish Congress, A&M Records, ABC News, Hallmark Cards, the U.S. Catholic Conference, and major league baseball's St. Louis Cardinals. The NRA's executive vice president stated, "Our members don't want to buy their songs, don't want to go to their movies, don't want to support their careers."

The Impact of Lobbying

The NRA is sometimes considered the best single-issue advocacy group in the United States. The organization boasts a large number of highly motivated members brought together by a common interest, who are willing to write letters, contribute money, attend meetings, and pressure politicians.

One of the earliest successful efforts of the "new" NRA occurred in 1982, when the organization spent more than $5 million to defeat California's Proposition 15. This ballot measure would have required the registration of all handguns and put a limit on the number of handguns in the state. Election Day polls revealed that while approximately 38 percent of the state's population owned guns, 48 percent of those who actually voted were gun owners.

Since that time, the NRA has been extraordinarily successful in motivating its members. For example, in the 2002 midterm elections, 230 of 246 House candidates endorsed by the NRA emerged victorious. The NRA does occasionally lose political battles, such as state referendums or the passage of the Brady Bill in 1993. However, the organization has succeeded in controlling the terms of the debate over guns in America by presenting firearms violence primarily as a crime issue and shifting the focus away from the country's gun manufacturers.

A poll taken in 2001 revealed that about half the American public thought the NRA had too much influence on gun control issues, compared to only 17 percent who claimed that it had too little influence. These numbers were unchanged since 1993. Not surprisingly, Americans who didn't own guns were far more likely to say that the NRA had too much influence—55 percent to 31 percent—whereas 43 percent of gun owners thought that the NRA's influence was about the right amount. The amount of power of the NRA is yet another disputed issue in the discussion of guns in America.

Movement of Gun Issues to the State Level

The hundreds of available results from state and national surveys over the last thirty years indicate that majorities in all states and time periods support almost all gun control measures except those calling for banning the sales or ownership of handguns. Most attitudes toward guns have changed very little, although there has been some increased support in most states for gun control measures, especially in the 1990s. Not surprisingly, support for gun

> **FAST FACT**
>
> In 2002, Colorado placed an initiative measure on the ballot to require background checks at gun shows. Supporters raised $848,000, including $115,000 from the Brady Campaign to Prevent Gun Violence (14 percent of the total); opponents raised $708,000, including $660,000 from the NRA (93 percent of the total). The measure passed by a large margin.

FAST FACT

The public occasionally votes directly on gun control measures in the form of referendums and initiatives, but these results have been inconclusive.

control is lowest in states and regions where recreational gun use and ownership are highest.

Not only have the Democrats failed to turn this pro-gun-control sentiment to their advantage, but the issue seems to have hurt them as much as it has helped them. Although Democrats have been the main supporters of firearms regulation, they lead the Republicans in public trust to handle the gun issue by only 46 percent to 40 percent. The long-standing political gridlock on this issue in Washington, D.C., however, has left a legislative void and resulted in the spread of the gun control debate downward to the state level.

CHAPTER 3

Guns and the Federal System

The Constitution of the United States, written in 1787, sets up a *federal* system. This means that power is divided between the state and national governments. The power of the national government is supreme; states cannot override national laws or the country would fall apart. Article VI of the Constitution contains what is known as the supremacy clause; it clearly states, "This Constitution, and the laws of the United States which shall be made in pursuance thereof; and all treaties made, or which shall be made, under the authority of the United States, shall be the supreme law of the land." For example, the national government is specifically responsible for foreign affairs and treaties, the military, coining money, and international trade policy.

Nonetheless, the U.S. Constitution reserves some powers of government for the states and smaller localities. This permits individual states to have some authority and

Statistically, more women than men support tighter gun control legislation, but those women who advocate gun use are a vocal minority. Sue Millsap and her family are pictured here in Charlotte, North Carolina, in 2000. Millsap, whose children have been taught to use and become comfortable with firearms, is a member of the Second Amendment Sisters, a group dedicated to preserving women's right to self-defense under the Second Amendment of the U.S. Constitution.

makes allowances for popular opinion and local feelings on specific issues. When the Constitution was written, Americans tended to view themselves as citizens of their states first and of the nation second—a situation that would last until the end of the American Civil War (1861–1865). The creators of the Constitution, having fought the American Revolution (1775–1783) to escape the tyranny of the British crown, had deliberately designed the federal system to check the power of a strong central government.

States traditionally are in charge of local matters, such as education and the ages at which residents can legally drink, drive, and marry; on such issues, states must be responsive to the wishes of their citizens. Gun regulations are also typically controlled by the state governments and not the U.S. Congress. In the twentieth century, however, the national government made great inroads into state powers in all areas, often by using the commerce clause of the Constitution (which deals with control of interstate trade).

Of course, the Second Amendment deals specifically with gun ownership. The Second Amendment was added to the Constitution in 1791 as part of a group of ten amendments known as the Bill of Rights. Like most of these amendments, the wording of the Second Amendment is quite brief. It has only one sentence: "A well regulated militia, being necessary to the security of a free State, the right of the people to keep and bear arms, shall not be infringed."

Unfortunately, there is not only dispute as to what this amendment means, but even whether the guarantees in the Bill of Rights apply to state laws at all. In a series of cases between 1920 and 1968, the U.S. Supreme Court interpreted the Fourteenth Amendment (ratified in 1868) to mean that state and local governments were bound by most of the restrictions that had applied all along to the federal government. However, not every part of the Bill of Rights has been officially applied to the states. On the few occasions—all in the nineteenth century—when the U.S. Supreme Court ruled on the meaning of the Second Amendment, it specifically refused to apply this amendment to the states.

Some people believe that Americans should simply assume that the Second Amendment applies to the states; they point to numerous Supreme Court decisions of the 1950s and 1960s in which restrictions against the power of the federal government were applied to the states. However, opponents note that the Supreme Court has never applied the Second Amendment to the states, despite many opportunities to do so. In recent decades, the Supreme Court has hesitated to extend any more protections from the Bill of Rights to the states, instead giving the individual states more leeway in making their own laws. The arguments over gun regulation have therefore drifted down from the national level to become a regular part of the politics of state, county, and municipal government. At these levels, local popular opinion plays an increasingly important part in the passage or rejection of legislation involving firearms.

Preemption

When the federal government takes away a state's right to make laws on a certain topic, it is using the legal doctrine known as *preemption*. Congress is permitted to preempt state or local governments in some cases because of the power given to it by the supremacy clause of the U.S. Constitution. However, the federal government rarely overrides local governments on firearms issues, even if those local regulations are stricter than current national law. State and local governments possess very broad powers to make laws and regulate in the interests of the public health, safety, and welfare. This is known as *police power.* Some of the largest states, including California, New York, New Jersey, Ohio, Massachusetts, and Illinois, also allow local governments a great deal of authority to regulate guns.

Oakland, California, councilman Henry Chang displays a small revolver during a news conference. Chang introduced legislation in 1996 to ban the sale of these cheap firearms, often referred to as junk guns, in the city of Oakland. Similar legislation has been challenged on the basis of preemption elsewhere in the state.

The issue of preemption also arises when local governments responding to the wishes of the people, such as in Los Angeles, California; New York City; and Chicago, Illinois, have tried to pass ordinances instituting stricter gun control than what exists on the state level. In most cases, the courts have supported local "home rule." A 1995 court decision, *Richmond Boro Gun Club, Inc. v. City of New York,* concluded that federal law did not cancel out an assault weapon ban instituted in New York City. In 2002, the California Supreme Court, holding that state law does not preempt the ordinances by Los Angeles County and Alameda County to regulate gun shows, rejected legal challenges to local firearms regulation.

In 1998, a California appeals court denied that state and national laws preempted a local ban on the sale of "junk guns" (cheap handguns) in *California Rifle & Pistol Association v. City of West Hollywood.* The court stated that although "something that is not prohibited by state law is lawful under state law...the Legislature [did not intend] to strip local governments of their constitutional power to ban the local sale of firearms which the local governments believe are causing a particular problem within their borders." However, because national, state, and local powers often overlap in the federal system, arguments over preemption tend to recur on the state and local level.

Some states have expressly removed the power of local governments to regulate firearms and reserved that power to the state governments. For example, a Minnesota law states that with a few exceptions,

> The legislature preempts all authority of a home rule charter or statutory city including a city of the first class, county, town, municipal corporation, or other governmental subdivision...to regulate firearms, ammunition, or their respective components to the complete exclusion of any order, ordinance or regulation by them.

United States v. Lopez

In 1992, Alfonso Lopez Jr. was a twelfth-grade student at Edison High School in San Antonio, Texas. On an anonymous tip, school authorities searched Lopez and discovered that he was carrying a .38-caliber handgun and five bullets. He was sentenced to six months in prison; his appeal eventually reached the Supreme Court. Lopez argued that the federal government had no authority to make laws regarding control of the public schools. His lawyers said that Congress was not using the commerce power of the Constitution properly when it passed the Gun-Free School Zones Act in 1990 to make gun possession on school grounds a federal crime. On April 26, 1995, a divided Supreme Court agreed, voting five to four to declare the law unconstitutional as an improper use of power by Congress. Chief Justice William Rehnquist, writing for the Court, stated that "the possession of a gun in a local school zone is in no sense an economic activity" that might have an effect on interstate commerce.

The decision in *Lopez* marked one of the few times since the 1930s that the Supreme Court declared a national law unconstitutional on the grounds that it violated states' rights. However, the concept became one of the basic principles of the Supreme Court under William Rehnquist, whose term as chief justice began in 1986. The decision in *United States v. Lopez* was another indication that the issue of regulation of gun possession would now be fought out at the state level.

> **FAST FACT**
>
> On the issue of gun-free school zones, more than forty states had passed legislation by 2003 outlawing possession of firearms on or near—usually within 1,000 feet (300 meters) of—school grounds.

Firearms in State Bills of Rights

The debate over the meaning of the Second Amendment to the U.S. Constitution has led people in many states to

Ron Straff, owner of R&R sporting goods store in Illinois, is just one of many business owners who would be affected by a lawsuit Mayor Richard M. Daley filed in 1998, accusing dealers and gun makers of creating a public nuisance with their products.

try to strengthen the rights of gun owners. In the last thirty years, at least fourteen states have either added "right to bear arms" clauses to their own state Bills of Rights for the first time or strengthened existing statements. These constitutional amendments took place in states such as Illinois, Virginia, Louisiana, Maine, and Nebraska. Some of these constitutional guarantees were exceedingly vague; for example, Illinois's stated only, "Subject only to the police power, the right of the individual citizen to keep and bear arms shall not be infringed." Others tried to be more specific; voters in Wisconsin in 1998 passed—by a 74 percent to 26 percent margin—a provision that said, "The people have the right to keep and bear arms for security, defense, hunting, recreation or any other lawful purpose."

Some states tried to write words into their state constitutions that they felt were missing in the U.S. Constitution. For example, North Dakota added a constitutional protection for the right to own firearms to

John W. Richardson, owner of Topeka Shooters' Supply in Topeka, Kansas, demonstrates a holster that could be used to carry a concealed weapon.

Article I, Section 1, of the state constitution in 1984.
It states:

> All individuals are by nature equally free and
> independent and have certain inalienable rights,
> among which are those of enjoying and defending
> life and liberty; acquiring, possessing, and
> protecting property and reputation; pursuing and
> obtaining safety and happiness; and to keep and
> bear arms for the defense of their person, family,
> property, and the state, and for lawful hunting,
> recreational, and other lawful purposes, which
> shall not be infringed.

However, like the Second Amendment to the U.S.
Constitution, even these wordier statements have been
interpreted by the courts to allow for firearms regulation.
In a 1987 North Dakota court case, a man was arrested,
charged, and convicted under a state law prohibiting the
possession of a firearm by a convicted felon. He challenged
the conviction, arguing that the law violated his new state
constitutional right to "keep and bear arms." The North
Dakota court concluded that the phrase "shall not be
infringed" should not be interpreted as preventing the
state legislature from placing any limits on the possession
of arms. The North Dakota court stated,

> We disagree with such a broad reading of the
> provision. Instead, we believe our Constitution's
> protection of the right to keep and bear arms is not
> absolute; although it prevents the negation of the
> right to keep and bear arms, that right nevertheless
> remains subject to reasonable regulation under the
> State's police power.

Private Gun Sales

One area where the national government has ceded
authority to the states is in the regulation of private gun
sales. The Gun Control Act of 1968 stated that persons

FAST FACT

Someone who buys a handgun from a "private" seller advertising in the newspaper can avoid the background check required of gun sales at stores. The *Sarasota Herald Tribune* in Florida stopped running classified gun advertisements after a convicted felon purchased a semiautomatic handgun from another individual through an advertisement in the paper and used the gun to murder his wife in front of her nine-year-old daughter.

"engaged in the business" of dealing in firearms must be licensed. In 1986, the McClure-Volkmer Act (also known as the Firearms Owners' Protection Act) defined the term "engaged in the business" to mean "a person who devotes time, attention, and labor to dealing in firearms as a regular course of trade or business with the principal objective of livelihood and profit through the repetitive purchase and resale of firearms." Congress specifically defined the term to exclude a person who "makes occasional sales, exchanges, or purchases of firearms for the enhancement of a personal collection or for a hobby, or who sells all or part of his personal collection of firearms."

A gun sale by anyone other than a federally licensed firearms dealer is known as a private, or secondary, sale. Federal law requires federally licensed firearms dealers to perform background checks on prospective firearms purchasers; maintain records of all gun sales; make those records available to law enforcement for inspection; report multiple sales; and report the theft or loss of a firearm from the licensee's inventory. However, federal law imposes none of these requirements on unlicensed sellers because private sellers are not subject to federal laws governing licensed dealers. As a result, private collectors or hobbyists can sell firearms without conducting background checks or keeping records of the sale in any way. Federal law does not even require private sellers to make sure that a buyer is old enough to purchase a gun. Not surprisingly, if convicted felons, minors, or other prohibited purchasers want guns, they usually turn to unlicensed sellers.

According to a 1999 report of the Bureau of Alcohol, Tobacco, and Firearms (BATF), the current definition of "engaged in the business" often makes it impossible for the government to prosecute "unlicensed dealers masquerading as collectors or hobbyists but who are really trafficking firearms to felons or other prohibited persons." The report recommended that Congress change the

definition of "engaged in the business" and require background checks on all gun show purchasers. As of 2003, these changes had not been made.

As a result, some states have responded to popular demand by passing laws to regulate the private sale of firearms. For example, California law states, "No person shall sell, lease, or transfer firearms unless he or she has been issued a license." However, there are numerous exceptions, such as if the seller is engaged only in "the infrequent sale, lease, or transfer of firearms."

Bob Baker (right), president and CEO of Freedom Arms, Inc., which manufactures high-end revolvers, with one of his employees at a gun show in Atlanta, Georgia, in 1999. The gun show loophole is a particularly difficult issue to combat because states must take upon themselves the regulation of the private sale of firearms if public opinion calls for it.

The Gun Show Loophole

The ability of private sellers to avoid following federal law regarding gun sales is known as the "gun show loophole" because the issue most frequently arises in connection with governmental regulation of gun shows. These shows feature the sale and display of firearms and firearms-related accessories. In the last few years, more than 4,000 gun shows were held each year in the United States, mostly in public spaces such as civic centers, fairgrounds, and armories. Most shows lasted two days, usually on weekends, and had anywhere from 50 to 2,000 display tables. These types of gun shows attracted an average of 2,500 to 5,000 people.

According to one BATF study, between a quarter and a half of the vendors at gun shows are unlicensed. Because federal law does not require unlicensed sellers to conduct background checks on prospective gun purchasers or to document firearms sales in any manner, gun shows are an easy source for illegal firearms sales throughout the United States. Gun shows have been the source of firearms

The 2000 Western Americana Gun Show in Pomona, California, was the last gun show held in Los Angeles County. In 1999, the board of supervisors in the district voted to ban shows on county property.

used in several tragic shootings, including the one at Columbine High School in Colorado. Based on BATF data for crimes committed in 1999, states without gun show background check requirements are supplying the nation with crime guns. Nearly half of the guns traced to crimes committed in states that require gun show background checks were originally purchased in other states (as compared to less than a quarter of guns traced to crimes committed in states that do not require background checks). When the BATF analyzed more than 1,500 gun trafficking investigations between July 1996 and December 1998, it concluded that gun shows were a "major trafficking channel" associated with approximately 26,000 illegally diverted firearms.

State Attempts to Close the Gun Show Loophole

In the absence of federal legislation, some states have responded to popular opinion by attempting to close the private sale loophole. In 1998, Florida voters overwhelmingly approved a referendum that would allow local authorities in Florida's counties to require background checks and waiting periods on sales by unlicensed dealers at gun shows. In California, all firearms sales, wherever they occur, must be conducted through a licensed dealer, or in counties of less than 200,000, through an authorized law enforcement agency. In 1999, the California legislature increased the state's overseeing of gun shows. New laws required gun show promoters to notify the state Department of Justice and local law enforcement of upcoming gun shows and proposed security plans for those shows. Promoters also had to guarantee that all firearms brought into the shows were cleared of ammunition and tagged for identification purposes, and prohibit anyone under eighteen from attending unless accompanied by a parent, grandparent, or legal guardian.

> **FAST FACT**
>
> Federal law defines a "gun show" as a "function sponsored by any national, state, or local organization devoted to the collection, competitive use, or other sporting use of firearms, or an organization or association that sponsors functions devoted to the collection, competitive use, or other sporting use of firearms in the community."

FAST FACT

Colorado's Amendment 22 was approved by more than 70 percent of the state's voters. Voters from rural counties in the eastern and western fringes of the state voted against the background check while the more urbanized Denver and Boulder areas strongly supported the amendment.

In 2000, voters in Colorado and Oregon easily passed specific measures to require background checks on purchasers of firearms at gun shows. The introductory text to Oregon's Measure 5 clearly stated,

> The laws of Oregon regulating the sale of firearms contain a loophole that allows people other than gun dealers to sell firearms at gun shows without first conducting criminal background checks. It is necessary for the safety of the people of Oregon that any person who transfers a firearm at a gun show be required to request a criminal background check before completing the transfer of the firearm.

Colorado's Amendment 22 also tried to eliminate the gun show loophole. The measure requires a designated licensed gun dealer to run background checks for unlicensed dealers at gun shows. A licensed dealer can charge the unlicensed dealer up to ten dollars per transaction for the service. The amendment also creates penalties for providing false information for the background check and failing to request a background check. Sellers of antique guns, however, are still not required to run a background check on buyers.

Gun Shows on Publicly Owned Property

State and local governments often rent out fairgrounds and civic centers to private organizations and use the money to support the purpose to which the property is devoted. In many parts of the country, publicly owned properties have become popular places for gun show operators, who lease the public property and then rent out space to sellers of firearms and ammunition, as well as other vendors. Given the problems associated with gun shows, some local governments, prodded by anti-gun advocates, have refused to allow their public spaces to be used for this purpose. Gun show operators have responded by asserting their right to free speech

In North Mankato, Minnesota, a sign maker examines some of his products that will be sold to local businesses and churches. A new handgun permit law allows organizations to post a sign if they want to keep handguns out of their buildings, an order that would then be enforceable by law.

guaranteed by the First Amendment to the U.S. Constitution. Although the sale and possession of guns and ammunition is not technically speech, people at gun shows may also exchange information and ideas, and the courts have ruled that the First Amendment traditionally protects these activities.

For example, the directors of an Ohio agricultural society that operated the Cuyahoga County Fairgrounds on behalf of the county refused to lease the county fairgrounds to a gun show promoter. The case was eventually settled out of court in favor of the gun show promoter. In a similar situation involving the "no gun" policy of the city-owned Century Center of South Bend, Indiana, a jury ruled that the gun show operator's First Amendment rights had been violated. Several other cases of this type have come up in California, where some local ordinances prohibit gun possession on county property or gun sales at county fairgrounds.

Some local governments in California and Illinois have attempted to directly impose regulations on gun shows. Los Angeles County, for example, adopted an ordinance in 1999 to prohibit the sale of firearms and ammunition on county-owned property, including the county fairgrounds. Los Angeles adopted this policy after agents from the Department of Justice easily bought numerous illegal weapons and accessories, including assault weapons, a rocket launcher, and several machine gun conversion kits, at a gun show held at the fairgrounds. In addition, the illegal firearms were immediately delivered to the agents in violation of state laws requiring background checks and a ten-day waiting period. Other California counties, such as Alameda in 1999 and Marin in 2003, adopted ordinances banning the possession of firearms and ammunition on county-owned property. Those policies were a response to a mass shooting at the Alameda County Fairgrounds that occurred during a county fair on July 4, 1998.

Registration

The registration of guns is another area where some states have acted in the absence of federal law. Not only is there no nationwide system of federal registration to track firearms ownership, but federal law specifically *prohibits* the creation of a national record of gun owners. However, although registration laws are prohibited at the federal level in the United States, opinion polls seem to show that the American public overwhelmingly favors such laws. Two separate polls in 2001 found that more than four out of every five Americans favor registration of all new handguns purchased.

Registration laws are supposed to provide the police with basic information about gun ownership. This would make it easier to trace guns involved in crimes and reduce illegal firearms sales by making gun owners accountable for each weapon. Opponents believe that registration is part of a plot to encourage more firearms prohibitions and eventually confiscate all the guns in the United States. As one gun advocate noted,

> Those who favor more gun control often accuse gun owners of being paranoid, but the track record of firearms registration is not a good one. Although there may be some benefit to firearms registration...the very real danger and potential for abuse that a firearm registration system presents [means that] gun rights activists will continue to vigorously oppose gun registration schemes.

On the state level, firearms registration requirements vary widely. When such laws exist, they usually require gun owners to register their firearms with the police or some other law enforcement agency by serial number and description. Whenever a gun is sold or given to someone else, the firearm must be registered again, and the police are supposed to be notified if the firearm is lost or stolen. In theory, gun owners have a great deal of incentive to follow these requirements, because in most states, if they fail to comply, they share some of the legal responsibility for any crimes or accidents involving their guns.

As is common in the nature of a federalist system, firearms registration requirements vary widely from state to state. Some states, such as Texas, Arizona, and Florida, have no registration requirements for either rifles or handguns. Others, such as Illinois, leave registration entirely up to city and local governments. In New York, handguns are registered, while handguns in Massachusetts are not registered—although their transfer is supposed to be recorded by the police. A few states, such as California and Hawaii, have laws requiring the maintenance of records of firearms purchasers. Washington, D.C., requires that anyone who owns a gun must hold a valid registration certificate.

FAST FACT

The state of Michigan does not directly register firearms owners, but requires all people who own handguns to present them for a safety inspection to local law enforcement. If the person presenting the handgun is eligible to possess it, a state certificate of inspection will be issued containing the name, age, address, description, and signature of the person, as well as a full description of the handgun. Copies of the certificate are kept by local law enforcement and the Michigan state police. Firearms dealers in Michigan must keep a register of all firearms sales.

Waiting Periods

In 1998, President Clinton assured former White House press secretary James Brady that Clinton would reject any legislation that would make it easier for criminals to obtain guns. The Brady Bill was named for Brady, a member of the Reagan administration, who had been shot in the assassination attempt on President Ronald Reagan in 1980.

Some states have passed laws requiring a waiting period, usually between two days and two weeks. This waiting period separates the time that a gun is purchased and the time that the purchaser can take actual physical possession of it. Waiting periods are intended not only to give law enforcement officials enough time to perform a background check on a purchaser, but also to provide a cooling-off period that might prevent impulsive acts of violence. Of course, U.S. law does not require private sellers to perform background checks on gun purchasers; this means that anyone buying a gun from a private seller can take immediate possession of the gun, unless state law provides otherwise.

The Brady Bill of 1993 required federally licensed firearms dealers to run a background check on gun purchasers or wait five business days before transferring a handgun to a buyer. Technically, this law does not ask for a true waiting period, because a dealer may transfer a firearm to a prospective purchaser as soon as he or she passes a background check; the delay is determined only by how long it takes to complete the check. By 1998, the Brady Bill had led to the establishment of the National Instant Criminal Background Check System (NICS). In the forty-nine months of operations between November 1998 (when the NICS began) and December 2003, the NICS processed more than 35 million background checks, resulting in more than 500,000 denials (between 1 percent and 2 percent of checks) of firearms purchases.

Waiting periods do not have universal support. One gun advocate noted that opposition to waiting periods and background checks was not "merely gun paranoia nonsense" but a reasonable response by some Americans to a fear that waiting periods are part of a broad campaign to ban guns altogether. He noted that waiting periods and background checks

> do appear to have merit since they will thwart some crime, and in most cases involve no practical infringement of law-abiding gun owners' rights.... So why do many gun rights groups resist all gun control measures?...the majority of citizens concerned about preserving gun rights would drop opposition to certain gun laws if the Second Amendment were treated as normal constitutional law.

Some states have their own waiting period requirements. For example, in Illinois, a buyer is required to show a Firearms Owner's Identification Card (FOID) when purchasing any firearms or ammunition. After a buyer applies to make a firearms purchase, a seller must withhold delivery of any handgun for seventy-two hours,

> **FAST FACT**
>
> The main reason for NICS denials of firearms purchases was the presence of a felony conviction in the purchaser's criminal history records (58 percent of denials). Another 14 percent of gun purchasers were denied for a misdemeanor crime of domestic violence, and 5 percent more were denied for a criminal record of drug abuse.

and of any rifle or shotgun for twenty-four hours. This state waiting period requirement does not apply to a buyer who is a dealer, law enforcement officer, or nonresident at a gun show recognized by the Illinois Department of State Police. The seller must keep a record of the transfer for ten years, including a description of the firearm, serial number, identity of the buyer, and buyer's FOID number.

Of course, the existence of waiting period legislation in state law books doesn't mean that the regulations are being taken seriously in the real world. Wal-Mart is the leading retailer of guns in the United States; most Wal-Mart stores sell long guns, but stores in Alaska sell handguns. In 2002, Wal-Mart began a new policy that required customers to undergo a background check before buying rifles and shotguns, no matter how long the check took. The action was taken after the retail chain's own research found that weapons it sold were being used in

In 2003, Wal-Mart, the leading retailer of guns in the United States, was forced to stop selling guns in its 118 California stores. State investigators had found at least 500 violations of state gun laws, most pertaining to improper background checks and violating waiting period regulations.

crimes. However, in April 2003, Wal-Mart was forced to temporarily stop selling guns at its 118 stores across California after state investigations revealed at least 500 violations of state gun laws in only six Wal-Mart stores. Among other violations, Wal-Mart employees sold shotguns to men convicted of spousal abuse and rifles to customers who had been convicted of felony drug charges. Clerks also failed to properly identify gun purchasers and delivered guns to buyers before the end of the required ten-day waiting period.

> **FAST FACT**
>
> An employee of Carter's Country, a Texas gun dealer, said that when customers admitted that they were felons, "we were directed on several occasions, find out if they've got somebody with them or can get somebody to come do the legal work to buy them the gun."

Referendums

States have occasionally allowed citizens to vote directly on certain gun control issues in the form of referendums or initiatives. These types of elections place an important political question before the entire electorate to be decided by a general vote. Because each referendum or initiative is unique—occurring in a specific state at a specific time and dealing with a uniquely worded question under distinct circumstances—the results tend to vary widely and are not always an accurate way to gauge the public's long-term opinion about firearms in America. Nonetheless, they provide an interesting snapshot of American opinion on gun control over the years. Some noteworthy referendums and initiatives involving firearms issues are listed below.

1976—Massachusetts: Voters emphatically rejected a ban on all handguns by a 69 percent to 31 percent margin out of approximately 2.4 million votes cast.

1982—California: Voters defeated Proposition 15, which would have required the registration of handguns and phased out handgun ownership through a permanent freeze on new sales and transfers. About 63 percent of Californians opposed the measure.

1988—Maryland: The Maryland legislature passed a law to prohibit future sales of "Saturday night specials," defining the only handguns to be banned as being too small and poorly made to be useful for self-defense or sport. Voters ratified the statute by a 57 to 42 percent margin.

1997—Washington: Voters overwhelmingly rejected Initiative 676, a gun control measure backed by billionaire Bill Gates that would have required state handgun owners to take safety tests and buy trigger locks in order to purchase handguns. The vote was 69 percent opposed and only 31 percent in favor of the initiative. Every county and demographic group voted against the proposed law.

1998—Florida: Voters overwhelmingly supported Revision 12, a referendum that allowed local authorities in Florida's counties to require background checks and waiting periods on sales by unlicensed dealers at gun shows. The state's vote to close the gun show loophole was a lopsided 72 percent to 28 percent.

1998—Wisconsin: More than 1.2 million people voted for a constitutional right-to-bear-arms amendment in 1998, while only 400,000 voted against it. The overwhelming 74 percent support included majorities in some urban and traditionally Democratic areas of Madison and Milwaukee.

1999—Missouri: Voters rejected a ballot initiative to repeal the state's concealed weapons ban by a 53 percent to 48 percent margin. Nearly every one of Missouri's rural counties voted to support the change, but city residents were overwhelmingly against the initiative. Suburban St. Louis County, a Republican stronghold, reported a surprising margin of 70 percent to 30 percent against the proposal.

2000—Oregon and Colorado: Voters overwhelmingly chose to close the gun show loophole by requiring background checks on all sales of firearms at gun shows. In both these western states with high rates of gun ownership, similar legislation had been narrowly defeated in the state legislature. Approximately 1.7 million Coloradans voted on Amendment 22, passing it by a 70 percent to 30 percent margin, while Oregon's Measure 5 passed 62 percent to 38 percent out of about 1.5 million votes cast.

At a rally for gun legislation in Denver, Colorado, in 2000, eight-year-old Jessie Hughes holds a sign showing the number of children killed by gunfire nationwide in one year.

Voters register to cast their ballots in Littleton, Colorado. In the wake of the Columbine High School massacre, voters in 2000 were able to place on the ballot a gun control measure that would require background checks for buyers at gun shows.

Although it is impossible to draw any firm conclusions from these results, taken as a whole, they do seem to imply that many polls overstate the degree of popular support for gun control measures. Gun advocates perceive a media plot that intentionally falsifies public opinion; gun control supporters believe that the polls are accurate but that the referendums do not reflect public opinion because of the immense power of the NRA and other lobbying organizations.

The Case of California

California has more people than any other state in the United States; almost one out of every ten Americans lives there. In most ways, it is not a typical state, but it has the reputation, perhaps undeserved, of being a trendsetter for the rest of the United States in both fashion and law. The regulation of firearms has increasingly become an issue in

California politics; by 2003, the state had some of the strictest gun regulations in the United States.

Californians have sent mixed messages on gun control. In 1982, a proposal to impose strict handgun controls and limit the number of handguns was crushingly defeated by a nearly two to one margin. In 1989, however, a gunman opened fire on a crowded elementary school playground in Stockton, California. The murderer used an AK-47 assault rifle fitted with a magazine holding seventy-five bullets; he killed five students and wounded thirty-three others before killing himself. As a result, California adopted legislation banning certain types of semiautomatic firearms. Known popularly as the Roberti-Roos Assault Weapons Act, after California legislators David Roberti and Mike Roos, this 1989 law served as a prototype for the national assault weapons ban of 1994.

In other attempts to reduce gun violence, the state of California and many of its cities and counties have experimented in diverse ways with gun regulation. They have passed bans on "junk guns," refused to permit gun shows on public property, required background checks on gun store employees, and forced private sellers to perform background checks. By 2003, individuals could purchase only one handgun every thirty days. All handgun sales had to include an approved firearm safety device, such as a trigger lock or safety box, for safe storage. California also passed legislation requiring new semiautomatic handgun models to have clear loaded-chamber indicators and magazine disconnect safeties. New guns must have one of the devices by 2006 and both by 2007.

State law required any person buying a gun to pass a thirty-question written test on gun laws and proper gun safety practices. The state legislature also required a prospective gun purchaser to perform a hands-on safety test demonstrating basic safe-handling knowledge to a Department of Justice certified instructor, including operation of the weapon's safety features, use of appropriate handgun safety locks, and proper loading and

Former California attorney general Bill Lockyer displays an illegally altered assault rifle that was sold at a gun show in 1999.

unloading practices. California laws also strengthened the background check by requiring a thumbprint and proof of state residency from all gun buyers.

The effect of these laws on the falling rate of gun crime and violence in California is disputed, of course, by the

opposing sides in the gun regulation debate. However, the laws do seem to have had some effect on the decrease in the number of guns in the state. When violent crime peaked in the state from 1992 to 1994, Californians purchased an average of 600,000 guns a year. In 2001, however, Californians purchased about 350,000 guns, pending a ten-day waiting period and background check of the buyer. The 155,203 handguns purchased in 2001 represented a thirty-year low, and the next year's figures were only slightly higher. With the exception of a higher number of gun purchases in 1999, gun purchases in California averaged about 350,000 a year from 1995 to 2002. During 2002, the California Department of Justice denied almost 4,000 sales because the purchaser fell into a prohibited category; about half of those denials were based on previous criminal convictions. California's attorney general noted, "We work not only to keep guns away from dangerous criminals, but also to make sure that law-abiding citizens are able to purchase, use, and store their firearms safely."

> **FAST FACT**
>
> In 2000, a California state court decisively ruled in *Kasler v. Lockyer* that "if plaintiffs are implying that a right to bear arms is one of the rights recognized in the California Constitution's declaration of rights, they are simply wrong. No mention is made in it of a right to bear arms."

The Laboratory of the States

In 1932, U.S. Supreme Court justice Louis Brandeis coined a famous phrase describing the American federalist system as a "laboratory of the states" in which state, city, and other local governments are given a free hand to experiment with various kinds of legislation, programs, and financing. Under the U.S. Constitution, the individual states are free to make their own decisions regarding what is best for their citizens. According to Brandeis, this freedom leads to a process of trial and error that will in the end uncover the best forms of government. This process is competitive because communities and states can take completely different approaches based on the varying forms that popular opinion takes in each state. Those localities whose policies prove effective serve as good examples to others, thereby improving public policy, while failed experiments are rejected.

Opponents of Brandeis's conception argue that giving more power to the states often leads to a "race to the bottom." States might provide the barest minimum required by Congress, rather than making serious attempts at new solutions to policy problems. Even worse, giving power to the popular majorities at the state level might lead to the denial of civil rights, as it did for African-Americans in the South for a hundred years after the Civil War.

The role of guns in American life is such a disputed issue that it has been almost impossible for gun control supporters to pass national legislation in Washington, D.C. Senator Charles Schumer, a staunch pro-gun control senator from New York, stated in 2003 that he still backed new gun laws but "we've had such a deadlock in Congress on this." Supporters of gun regulations have instead turned to the "laboratory of the states" to try to regulate guns and gun ownership. The result has been a patchwork of state and local laws in which some areas have absolutely no limits and some have serious restraints.

Such a situation, of course, is not unique to gun legislation—the driving age and high school graduation requirements, among numerous other things, vary from state to state. Law enforcement officials have long been familiar with the problems caused by such varying laws. For example, if one state sets the minimum age to drink alcohol at eighteen and a neighboring state sets it at twenty-one, underage drinkers from the more restrictive state will simply travel to the less restrictive state in order to purchase alcohol. In the case of beverage alcohol, the federal government intervened in 1984 and passed the National Minimum Drinking Age Act, which required all states to raise their minimum purchase and public possession of alcohol age to twenty-one. States that did not follow this law faced a reduction in highway funds under the Federal Highway Aid Act. By 1988, every state had a minimum legal drinking age of twenty-one.

Former California governor Gray Davis signed into law in 1999 a series of bills imposing strict regulations on the sale and ownership of firearms. In this photograph, he stands beside a barrel holding 280 handguns, signifying the average number of handguns confiscated by Los Angeles police in one month.

No such nationwide solution seems likely in the realm of gun regulation. The lack of agreement in Washington, D.C., is mirrored by the lack of agreement in the nation as a whole. The federalist system has merely moved the debate over guns and regulation to a decentralized setting. Rather than serve as experiments in public policy that citizens can logically and carefully assess, the varying state and local gun control regulations have proved every bit as contentious as the same arguments on the national level. There is no agreement as to which policies have value, let alone which policies work, and so the debate rages on. In this way, gun control legislation represents both the best and worst aspects of the federal system.

CHAPTER 4

Crime and Self-Defense

I n the 1970s and 1980s, the crime rate began to rise extremely rapidly in the United States. The homicide rate for all Americans (measuring the number of people murdered each year) doubled from the mid-1960s to the late 1970s. In 1980, it peaked at 10.2 per 100,000 people and subsequently fell off to 7.9 per 100,000 in 1985. It rose again in the late 1980s and early 1990s to another peak in 1991 of 9.8 per 100,000.

The quantity and usage of guns seemed to play a major role in the rise of the crime rate. Between 1985 and 1991, the homicide rate for adolescents under eighteen tripled, and the number of gun-related homicides more than doubled, yet there was no accompanying growth in nongun homicides. Similar statistics appeared in analysis of robberies; from 1989 to 1991, the total rate of robberies using firearms increased by 42 percent, while the rate of robberies without firearms increased by only 5 percent.

Beginning in the early 1990s, however, the crime rate began to decrease at an extraordinary rate for all ages. The homicide rate alone dropped more than 25 percent between 1993 and 1998, from near-historic highs to thirty-year lows. By 2003, homicide rates had fallen to levels last seen in the late 1960s. This dramatic decrease was almost entirely the result of a decrease in crimes committed with guns. Between 1993 and 1998, gun-related crime dropped more than 30 percent, and the number of juvenile gun homicide offenders fell 57 percent. Violent crime rates, which include rape, robbery, aggravated assault, and homicide, also declined for all age groups between 1993 and 2001. The homicide rate for all Americans dropped to 6.3 per 100,000 in 1998, 5.7 in 1999, and 5.5 in 2000, and then rose slightly to 5.6 in 2001. According to the Department of Justice's National Crime Victimization Survey (NCVS) in 2002, violent crime rates had declined so greatly since 1994 that they reached the lowest level ever recorded by the survey. In addition, the 2002 survey noted that the property crime rate had dropped continuously for the past twenty years.

Many causes have been suggested for the huge drop in crime in the United States since 1990. These explanations include an improved economy, an aging population, the stabilization of the crack cocaine trade in large cities, the Brady Bill of 1993, the easing of concealed handgun restrictions, improvements in violence prevention programs, tougher sentencing, and increased numbers of police. Whatever the main reason or reasons, the dramatic rise and fall of the crime rate has greatly affected the debate over the role of guns in American life. Whether the crime rate is rising or falling, however, gun advocates argue that firearms are crucial to protecting oneself in the United States, while supporters of gun regulations emphasize the role of guns in the committing of crimes.

There is much controversy over how big a role the media play in the connection between guns and violence. In the 1980s, actor Charles Bronson starred in the series of Death Wish *films that glorified the act of an ordinary citizen taking the law into his own hands.*

Death Wish

The rising crime rate of the 1970s and 1980s focused a good deal of the public's attention on the seeming

FAST FACT

The number of law enforcement officers killed in the line of duty has declined since the 1970s; 644 officers were killed in the ten years between 1991 and 2000, compared to 1,085 between 1973 and 1982. More than 90 percent of murdered law enforcement officers are killed with firearms—particularly handguns.

inadequacies of the police in preventing crime. After the race riots of the 1960s, the military defeat in the Vietnam War (1964–1975), and the revelation of vast government corruption in the Watergate scandal from 1972 to 1974, many Americans began to distrust traditional government institutions such as the army and the police.

In 1973, Al Pacino starred in the film *Serpico*, based on the true story of Frank Serpico, a New York City police

Former New York City undercover police officer Frank Serpico in 1998.

officer who fought corruption in the department. The popular movie portrays most police officers as either uncaring or corrupt. The movie reinforced the belief of some Americans, following the nation's individualist creed, that, in the end, citizens had to be responsible for protecting themselves. Supporters of this view held that there should be few or no restrictions on a person's ability to own or carry a gun.

In 1974, the controversial movie *Death Wish* became an American blockbuster and a topic of conversation throughout the nation. In the film, an architect (played by Charles Bronson) throws off his everyday life and takes the law into his own hands after criminals murder his wife and rape his daughter. He becomes a *vigilante*, a person who claims to be personally enforcing justice because there are no effective legal or enforcement organizations. Seeking vengeance, Bronson's mythic character attempts to rid the city of criminals; this urban warrior seems to go on a killing spree every time he leaves the house, while the police are portrayed as either useless or an actual hindrance to law and order.

The architect's executions of criminals brought cheers from crime-weary audiences in the 1970s. Some people, however, criticized the movie for exploiting urban fears about crime, while others saw it as nothing more than a mindless action film. Although the main character's vigilantism brought widespread criticism, *Death Wish* became one of the big moneymakers of the year, and Bronson made *Death Wish* sequels in 1982, 1985, 1987, and 1994. He defended them by noting, "I think they provide satisfaction for people who are victimized by crime and look in vain for authorities to protect them. But I don't think people try to imitate that kind of thing."

"The Subway Vigilante"

Some movies borrow a great deal from real-life incidents, but sometimes real events seem to be based on movies. On the afternoon of December 22, 1984, four African-American

> **FAST FACT**
>
> The inability of the police to protect Americans remains a major argument for those who oppose gun regulations. For example, one gun advocate stated that "citizens truly concerned with their safety will seek the appropriate training.... It is extremely doubtful that the police will be there to protect you if you are the victim of a crime—they will most likely show up minutes, or even hours later to take a statement or fill out a report. If confronted by someone who plans to rape or murder you, which do you prefer: Having an immediate means of self-defense (a pistol, a knife, a stun gun—anything!) or having a police officer picking up the pieces?"

youths boarded an express subway train in New York City on a mission to rob video game machines in lower Manhattan. While about twenty other passengers in the car watched, they surrounded Bernhard Goetz, a small, white, thirty-six-year-old electronics engineer. One asked Goetz for five dollars; Goetz acted as if he didn't hear him and asked him to repeat his request. The youth responded, "Give me your money." Goetz stood up, drew a revolver from inside his jacket, and fired shots at the youths. All four were hit and, as one lay bleeding, Goetz reputedly said, "You don't look too bad, here's another," and shot him again. The last shot severed his spinal cord and left him paralyzed. Goetz escaped through the opening between two cars and fled to Vermont; he surrendered to police nine days later.

Goetz's actions brought the debate over legitimate self-defense into the center of American life. The four young

The Bernhard Goetz case is an example of how public attitudes toward gun control can change over the years. In 1984, when the crime rate was soaring in New York City, Goetz (pictured here) was acquitted of the shooting on grounds of self-defense. Twelve years later, when city crime levels were drastically reduced, Goetz was hit with a $43 million civil penalty for acting recklessly.

men, all eighteen or nineteen at the time, claimed at first that they were panhandling money to play video games and had merely asked Goetz for five dollars. Two of the four were carrying screwdrivers inside their jackets at the time of the shooting, which they later admitted they intended to use to break into the coin boxes of video game machines. Goetz maintained that he believed he was being robbed and threatened.

Although Goetz confessed to the shooting, a New York jury acquitted him of the shooting on the grounds of self-defense and convicted him only on charges of illegal possession of a firearm. For this crime, Goetz was sentenced to eight months in prison. In 1996, a full twelve years later, a jury, finding that Goetz had acted recklessly, awarded the paralyzed youth $43 million in damages ($18 million for past and future pain and suffering and $25 million in punitive damages). Shortly afterward, Goetz filed for bankruptcy. The other three young men have all committed other crimes since the incident.

The rise in crime and incidents such as the subway vigilante case popularized the idea that people might need to carry or own guns in order to defend themselves. The sale of handguns skyrocketed, even overtaking rifle and shotgun sales in some years. Handguns represented only about one-fifth of all guns purchased in America in the 1950s; until 1967, handgun sales had never totaled more than 700,000 in any year. From 1982 to 1993, however, Americans bought approximately 50 million guns, of which about 20 million were handguns; handgun sales exceeded 2 million every year between 1979 and 1982. Approximately one-third of the guns owned by Americans are handguns; they continue to be the weapon of choice for both self-defense and crime.

Justifiable Homicide

The subway vigilante case raised the question, under what circumstances is it legal and/or acceptable to use a gun in self-defense? A *justifiable homicide* occurs when one person kills another person to prevent a felony, and the law considers it legally permissible. Anywhere in the United States, people are within their rights under the law to use deadly force to protect themselves or someone else from death or serious bodily harm. However, the term "justifiable homicide" is interpreted slightly differently from state to state. In some states, the law assumes that someone breaking into a house or apartment intends to do serious bodily harm; therefore, people are justified in shooting anyone who breaks into their residence. In general, however, "justifiable homicide" means the killing of an assailant in self-defense and as a last resort. For example, shooting someone for stealing a car is not considered justifiable homicide (unless someone's life is in danger).

Justifiable homicides are extremely rare in the United States, averaging only 176 occurrences per year for the five years between 1997 and 2001. This is less than 2 percent of all recorded homicides in the United States. The FBI gives statistics for the number of justifiable homicides by private citizens.

Because "justifiable homicide" in the United States is a narrowly defined legal term, the number of actual occurrences is probably undercounted, although whether just by a few homicides (according to gun control supporters) or by an enormous number (according to gun advocates) is the subject of debate.

Year	Justifiable Homicides	Justifiable Firearms Homicides	Total Homicides	Percentage of Total Homicides That Are Justifiable Firearms Homicides
1997	280	238	10,729	2.2 percent
1998	196	170	9,257	1.8 percent
1999	192	158	8,480	1.9 percent
2000	164	138	8,661	1.6 percent
2001	215	176	8,719	2.0 percent

Guns and Justifiable Homicide

Not surprisingly, handguns were by far the weapon most commonly used in recorded justifiable homicides between 1997 and 2001. Because they can be concealed, handguns were the weapon of choice in four out of every five justifiable homicides. However, the total number represents only about one out of every fifty handgun homicides.

Guns and Self-Defense

If fatally shooting an attacker was the only way that a gun could prevent crime, then carrying one would be next to worthless, since homicides outnumber justifiable homicides by almost fifty to one. However, the owner of a gun might prevent crime in other ways—for example, by wounding an attacker, firing warning shots, or simply waving the gun and scaring off the criminal. Unfortunately, the number of times that firearms are used in this manner for self-defense is even harder to determine than justifiable homicide and subject to even greater controversy. The number of people killed and injured with firearms is fairly accurately known, but the number of criminals scared off by law-abiding citizens showing firearms (without using them) is impossible to prove.

Year	Justifiable Homicides with Firearms	Justifiable Handgun Homicides	Percentage of Justifiable Firearm Homicides That Are Justifiable Handgun Homicides	Homicides with Handguns	Percentage of Handgun Homicides That Are Justifiable Handgun Homicides
1997	238	197	83 percent	8,441	2.3 percent
1998	170	150	88 percent	7,430	2.0 percent
1999	158	137	87 percent	6,658	2.1 percent
2000	138	123	89 percent	6,778	1.8 percent
2001	176	136	77 percent	6,790	2.0 percent

Retired Minneapolis police officer Gary Bjergo offers a course in the legal technicalities of self-defense as part of a training effort to prepare people for carrying concealed guns in Minnesota.

Some gun owners are likely to exaggerate their heroism by overreporting firearms use in self-defense, while others may underreport firearms use for fear of becoming involved in a police investigation.

At the virtual peak of the crime wave, the NCVS, organized by the U.S. Department of Justice, reported on the issue of defensive gun usage. It asserted,

> In 1992, offenders armed with handguns committed a record 931,000 violent crimes. Handguns accounted for about 13 percent of all

violent crimes.... On average in 1987–1992 about 83,000 crime victims per year used a firearm to defend themselves or their property. Three-fourths of the victims who used a firearm for defense did so during a violent crime; a fourth, during a theft, household burglary, or motor vehicle theft.... 38 percent of the victims defending themselves with a firearm attacked the offender, and the others threatened the offender with the weapon.

According to the NCVS, the number of times that firearms were used for self-defense in 1992 was three times greater than that year's murder rate. However, the number of murders was only about 1 percent of the total number of robberies and assaults for the year. In 1993, the NCVS estimated that offenders armed with guns committed a record 1.3 million violent crimes. Because the NCVS claimed that guns were used in self-defense approximately 83,000 times a year, this meant that firearms were over sixteen times more likely to be used in a crime than in defense. If these data were accurate, handgun ownership had been vastly oversold as a way to defend oneself against "bad guys"; instead, an increase in handguns meant an increase in crime. Needless to say, the NCVS statistics quickly came under attack by gun advocates.

The National Crime Victimization Surveys

Most of the disputes over defensive gun use eventually run into the issue of the accuracy of the NCVS. Actually, the U.S. Department of Justice also collects another, slightly different set of statistics to measure the amount, nature, and impact of crime in the United States: the Uniform Crime Reporting (UCR) program. The UCR program, which began in 1929, collects crime information from monthly law enforcement reports given directly to the FBI. In 2001, the UCR crime reports covered about 90 percent of the total population, but its statistics are totally dependent on crimes reported to the police.

Dissatisfaction with the accuracy and limitations of the UCR caused the Department of Justice's Bureau of Statistics to create the NCVS in 1973 (redesigned in 1993). Thirty years old, this crime statistics survey is the second-largest ongoing survey in the United States and is meant to fill in the gaps of the UCR. The NCVS is currently organized so that, twice a year, U.S. Census Bureau personnel interview household members in a nationally representative sample of approximately 42,000 households (about 76,000 people). More than 150,000 interviews of Americans age twelve or older are conducted every year. Households stay in the sample for three years, and new households are constantly rotated into the sample. The NCVS furnishes previously unavailable information about crime—for example, crimes not reported to the police—as well as information about specific groups in the population, such as women, the elderly, members of various racial minorities, and city dwellers. The NCVS provides a way for victims to describe the impact of crime and the characteristics of violent offenders.

Unlike the UCR, the NCVS doesn't rely on victims to report crimes to the police but asks people directly what crimes have happened to them. Because it doesn't rely on the law enforcement agencies, there's no temptation to "improve" the crime figures for public relations reasons, such as to make the police look more effective. In addition, by asking victims to identify the characteristics of the criminals who injured them, the NCVS doesn't suffer from the problem of racial bias by police or prosecutors (although there is the possibility that the statistics might be skewed by racial bias on the part of the victims). The NCVS surveys a large number of people but still has the resources to analyze very detailed responses involving whether the respondent fought back, if a weapon was used, and if injuries resulted from the encounter. Most of the surveys are conducted over the phone, and the law guarantees a participant's anonymity.

The NCVS between 1993 and 2001 boasted response rates between 93 percent and 96 percent of eligible households (out of more than 300,000) and 89 percent to 92 percent of eligible individuals (out of more than 650,000).

Gun Advocates Dispute the NCVS Figures

The NCVS is generally considered the most authoritative source on the criminal and defensive uses of guns. However, gun advocates have strongly denounced it as untrustworthy or inaccurate, particularly because they feel that the NCVS uses poor methods to gather its statistics. To begin with, murder victims can't fill out surveys, so the NCVS can't acquire any meaningful data about homicides. Because the surveys cover a six-month period, participants may forget about crimes that they reported to their local police. Some studies seem to indicate that some groups, such as African-Americans, may underreport minor crimes to the NCVS.

Here is an example of the results of a National Crime Victimization Survey showing the decline in violent crime rates between 1973 and 1998. Opponents of gun control cite the inaccuracy of the NCVS's reporting techniques to bolster their arguments against stricter gun control.

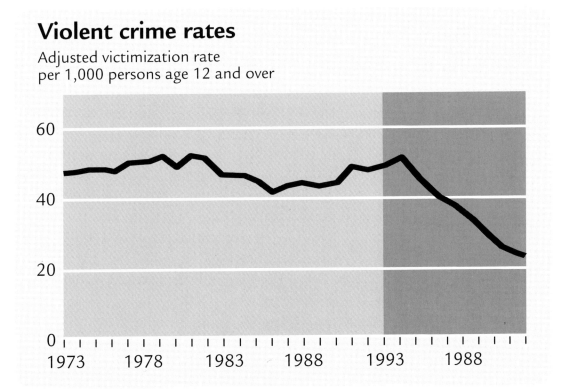

Violent crime rates
Adjusted victimization rate
per 1,000 persons age 12 and over

This picture of a woman holding a handgun might influence others to carry firearms in order to defend themselves against crime because the subject appears strong, empowered, and in control.

Opponents of gun control claim that the survey severely undercounts the number of times that victims use guns against their attackers. Gun advocates imply that perhaps twenty-nine out of thirty respondents who use guns in self-defense do not tell the NCVS of this fact, for several reasons. Most importantly, the NCVS never asks people directly whether they used a gun in self-defense. In some cases, the respondent possessed or was using the gun illegally. In other cases, the respondents simply think that they possessed or were using the gun legally but are not completely sure and have no desire to be investigated further. In addition, gun advocates believe that many people who use guns to protect themselves successfully don't consider themselves victims and are not counted by the study. One pro-gun researcher asserted, "The one survey that is clearly not suitable for estimating the total number of defensive gun uses is the NCVS."

In 1991, gun advocate Gary Kleck cited figures that he said showed that Americans defended themselves with firearms 1 million to 2 million times a year and that the use of guns saved thousands of lives a year. In 1995, Kleck—citing further studies—made his claim more precise, implying that firearms were used for self-protection an astonishing 2.5 million times annually (as opposed to less than 100,000 times in the NCVS count). He not only reasserted this figure in a book in 1997, but called it a conservative estimate and speculated that the actual number was much higher.

For 1992, Kleck concluded that there were 2.4 million successful gun defenses—1.9 million of them with handguns—and that about 72 percent of these gun defenses occurred in or near the home. Kleck speculated that the reason the expected nonfatal firearms injuries implied in his study did not show up in the medical data was that most of those wounded did not seek medical attention. If these results are correct, guns are used for protection and self-defense far more often than in criminal activities. Therefore, the purchase of a gun would be a worthwhile investment, and an increase in firearms would be a positive movement in American life.

Needless to say, these controversial statements have produced numerous counterstudies by other researchers who have criticized the methods and conclusions of Kleck's publications. Kleck's numbers differed enormously from the results of the NCVS, which indicated that the number of gun crimes (about 850,000 in 1996) was about twelve times higher than the number of defensive gun uses (about 72,000 in 1996). The respondents in Kleck's survey, however, reported 2.5 million defensive gun uses. Kleck also claimed that the NCVS vastly undercounts the number of robberies, as well as defensive gun uses.

Weapon Use and Violent Crime from 1993 to 2001

Between 1993 and 2001, the NCVS interviewed more than 650,000 individuals over the age of eleven in more than 300,000 households. The results indicate that between 1993 and 2001, there were an estimated 8.9 million violent crimes committed in the United States. About a quarter of these crimes were committed by offenders armed with any weapon, such as a gun or knife. About 800,000 of these incidents, or about 10 percent of the grand total, involved a criminal with a firearm. Between 1993 and 2001, victims were confronted by offenders armed with guns in about 27 percent of robberies, 8 percent of assaults, and 3 percent of all sexual assaults.

NCVS statistics also indicate that between 1993 and 2001, about 61 percent of all victims of violent crime reported taking some type of defensive measure during the incident. Most victims did little more than try to

VICTIMS' RESPONSES TO VIOLENT CRIMES	
Offered no resistance	39.3 percent
Method of resistance unknown	0.2 percent
Took some action	60.5 percent
Resisted or captured offender	15.0 percent
Scared or warned off offender	4.2 percent
Persuaded or appeased offender	5.5 percent
Escaped/hid/got away	9.8 percent
Got help or gave alarm	3.9 percent
Reacted to pain or emotion	0.3 percent
Other	8.9 percent
Used physical force toward offender	13.0 percent
Attacked/threatened offender without weapon	10.8 percent
Attacked/threatened offender with gun	0.7 percent
Attacked/threatened offender with other weapon	1.4 percent

escape, get help, or attempt to scare or warn off the attacker. Approximately 13 percent of victims of violent crime tried to attack or threaten the offender; only about 2 percent of victims of violent crime used a weapon to defend themselves, and in only half these cases—about 1 percent—did violent crime victims show or use a firearm.

The NCVS estimated the average annual number of violent victimizations by an offender with a firearm at 850,000 and reported about 62,000 cases of self-defense with firearms each year. For the years 1993 to 2001, then, the NCVS report shows that these weapons are overwhelmingly used more for crime than self-defense.

For example, according to the NCVS, in 1998, there were only 170 justifiable homicides committed by private citizens using firearms in the United States. Of these, 150 involved handguns. While firearms sometimes are used by private citizens to kill criminals or to prevent crimes, guns are far more often used for suicide (17,424 in 1998), homicide (12,102 in 1998), or even fatal unintentional

Virginia Velezquez of Brooklyn, New York, demonstrates how she frightened would-be robbers from her store by defending herself with a licensed firearm she keeps for just such purposes. Many small-business owners believe that the right to defend themselves is vital to their safety and security.

injury (866 in 1998). In 2000, 64 percent of all homicides and 57 percent of all suicides in the United States resulted from the use of firearms.

Women and Justifiable Homicide

There is a definite difference between male and female attitudes toward guns. A 1996 study estimated that only 7 percent of women owned a handgun—less than one out of every ten women. Of these handgun-owning women, however, more than four-fifths claimed to own their firearms for self-defense purposes. Women make up half of the population of the United States but commit only 9 percent of murders, are arrested for spousal abuse in less than 5 percent of cases, and are virtually never accused of rape. More than nine out of ten rapists, murderers, and batterers in the United States are men. In general, handguns are meant to be aimed at humans; a woman buys a handgun because she envisions protecting herself against a male attacker.

This photograph shows a member of Second Amendment Sisters preparing for gun practice.

Guns are durable products that rarely break unless harshly mistreated. For that reason, gun manufacturers need to find new buyers in order to stay in business. Since at least 1980, the firearms industry, seeing women as a vast untapped market, has attempted to promote gun sales to women in the interest of self-defense. In advertisements, gun manufacturers focus on the threat of attack by a stranger; a woman is depicted alone and vulnerable, perhaps walking on a dark street or at home asleep. Her attacker, according to this stereotypical image, is a stranger who will rape, rob, and eventually kill her. Because fear sells handguns, firearms manufacturers emphasize the insecurity and victimization of women; gun publications are filled with images of women armed with handguns, fighting off attackers.

In fact, lone male attackers do often kill women. According to one gun advocacy group, in 1998, there were 1,932 women murdered by men in cases involving one female homicide victim and one male offender. However, these attackers were rarely strangers or deranged maniacs. In 1998, more than ten times as many women were murdered by a man whom they knew (1,699 victims) than were killed by male strangers (138 victims). Nearly six out of every ten female homicide victims were either the wives, girlfriends, friends, or acquaintances of their killers. In 2000, the number of females shot and killed by their husbands or intimate acquaintances was almost four times higher than the number murdered by male strangers using all weapons combined.

There were 410 women shot and killed—more than one woman a day—by either a husband or close friend during the course of an argument. In more than 80 percent of all incidents in 1998 where circumstance could be determined, homicides were not related to any other crime such as rape or robbery. The offender is known to the victim in almost three-quarters of all sexual assaults in the United States, and six out of every ten sexual assaults in the United States happen to children and adolescents under eighteen. In 1998, for every time a woman used a handgun to kill an intimate acquaintance in self-defense, eighty-three women were murdered by an intimate acquaintance with a handgun.

Of course, the same limitations work against these statistics as against the earlier ones for general defensive gun usage. Without a consensus on how many times a woman waves a gun and scares off an attacker, it's next to impossible to determine whether carrying a gun might be a good investment for a woman. Because most women are threatened by acquaintances and family members and not strangers in the street, gun control supporters believe that gun advocates who advise women to buy firearms to repel their enemies are selling a fantasy rather than a solution. According to this view, husbands and boyfriends who parade in public as decent, law-abiding men can often be domestic batterers and wife-beaters in private. Any gun that a woman keeps inside her house for self-defense is more likely to be used to threaten or even kill the woman herself.

On the other hand, gun advocates point out that women are capable of making informed choices to defend themselves. In addition to repelling the danger of attacks by strangers, a gun might be useful for a woman even against an attack by someone whom she knows—for example, if a woman leaves her abusive husband but finds herself being stalked by him.

Guns, Crime, and Self-Defense in the Early Twentieth Century

Despite the enormous drop in crime, the United States remained a violent country in the first years of the twenty-first century, especially compared with other industrialized nations in Europe and Asia. The FBI's *Crime in the United States* reported that 63 percent of the 15,980 murders in 2001 were committed with firearms (in 2000, the number was 66 percent of 15,517 murders) while forty-seven of the fifty-one law enforcement officers killed in the line of duty in the United States died from gunshot wounds. Homicides and firearms violence remain heavily concentrated in urban areas; more than half of all U.S. homicides occur in sixty-six cities, with more than 20 percent in the top ten. Gun-related crime is a particularly serious problem in public housing, despite the falling crime rate; the 2.6 million people living in public housing are twice as likely to suffer from firearms-related victimization as other members of the population.

In Macoupin County, Illinois, the local police force responded to community requests to offer a class teaching women how to handle guns for self-defense purposes only. It has been extremely popular with women of all ages.

According to the NCVS, in 2002, more than 300,000 victims of serious violent crimes (rape, sexual assault, robbery, and aggravated assault) stated that they faced an offender with a firearm. This number represented 7 percent of the 5.3 million violent crimes (down from 8 percent of 6.3 million in 2000). Although the number of gunshot wounds from assaults treated in hospital emergency departments fell from 64,100 in 1993 to 39,400 in 1997 (a 39 percent decline), more than 100 patients are still treated for gunshot trauma in the United States every day. Many American homes contain guns, almost half of all homicides and suicides occur in a home, and the majority of victims are shot with guns. Areas with high gun ownership rates seem to have the highest rates of gun-related mortality.

On the other hand, most people who buy a handgun—more than 1 million Americans every year—believe that it will protect their homes and families. This practice is defended by citing evidence that persons frequently and effectively use guns to keep from being attacked and killed. The question of whether gun ownership has a net benefit or risk in the area of self-defense remains an issue of the greatest controversy.

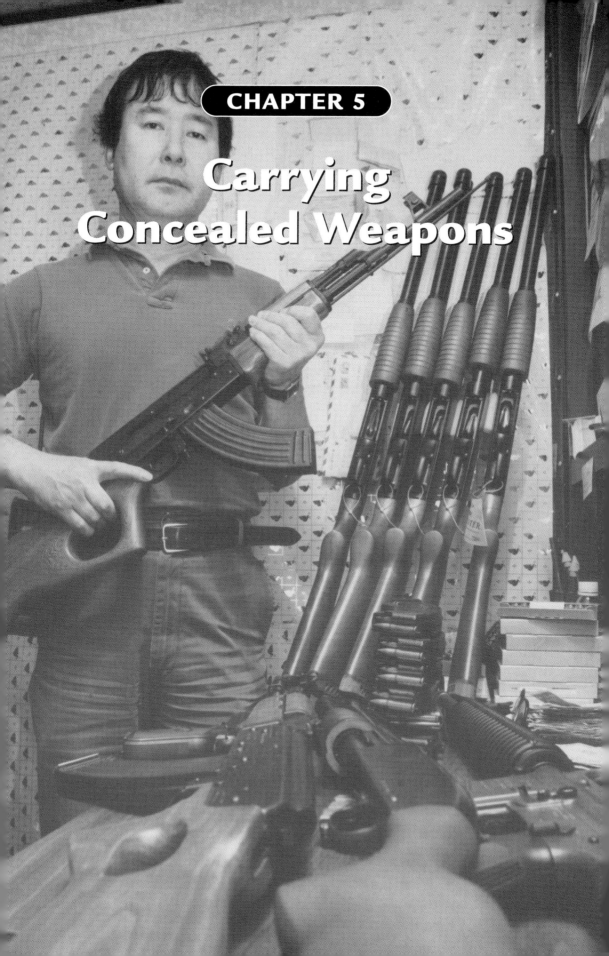

CHAPTER 5

Carrying Concealed Weapons

I n the 1800s, most states in the United States banned the carrying of concealed weapons in the interest of public safety. Nineteenth-century Americans believed that the chances of violence increased as the number of people who carried concealed weapons increased; the danger to society more than canceled out any possible benefits that could be gained through more effective individual self-defense. As of the mid-1980s, only ten states allowed all their citizens to acquire a permit to carry a concealed gun. The remaining states either entirely banned carrying concealed firearms or gave sheriffs and other police officials a great deal of discretion to decide who could and couldn't carry concealed weapons. For example, law enforcement officials could reject requests to carry concealed weapons using such vague guidelines as whether the applicant possessed "good character" or was a potential threat to public safety.

The rising crime rate after 1970 changed this traditional attitude. Many Americans became convinced that they could rely not on the police for protection, but only on their own wits and abilities. A movement sprang up to loosen concealed-carry laws so that gun owners would be permitted to carry concealed and loaded weapons in public. Supporters argued that because criminals were carrying concealed and loaded weapons, law-abiding gun owners should have the right to protect themselves. That way, people could defend themselves when the police were unavailable.

Beginning in the late 1980s, there was an enormous increase in the number of states that allowed carrying concealed weaponry. This trend continued even as the crime rate fell dramatically in the late 1990s. While American firearms legislation became somewhat stricter on the national level with the passage of the Brady Bill in 1993 and the assault weapons ban of 1994, it became more permissive on the state level. For example, in 1995, Texas overturned the state's 125-year ban on concealed weapons; Governor George W. Bush signed the bill into law. The state further amended the law in 1997 to permit Texans to carry concealed weapons in churches, amusement parks, hospitals, and nursing homes and allow people with carrying concealed weapons (CCW) permits from other states to carry concealed weapons in Texas. By 2000, more than 200,000 Texans had received permits to carry concealed and loaded guns in public places.

Like many issues pertaining to guns in America, the carrying of concealed and loaded firearms in public places is extremely controversial. Supporters and opponents of CCW laws often seem to be talking past each other rather than to each other. This is because they begin from completely different first principles; where supporters see improved personal and national safety, opponents see increased gun violence. Americans are sharply divided on the basic question of whether concealed-carry weapons make life safer by allowing citizens to arm themselves against possible criminals, or more dangerous by increasing the number of armed people out and about in

The controversial debate over citizens' rights to carry concealed weapons was at issue in Cincinnati, Ohio, in 2003, when approximately fifty people marched through neighborhoods wearing holstered weapons and gun belts. The march had been organized in support of a lawsuit to overturn a state ban on concealed weapons.

public. A 2001 poll found Americans split almost exactly evenly on a ban on carrying concealed weapons; 49 percent supported the idea, and 48 percent opposed it. Another survey reported that 56 percent of Americans believe that CCW permits should be issued only to those law-abiding adults who can prove "special needs" to carry.

"Shall Issue" and "May Issue"

There is no national law that regulates the carrying of concealed weapons in any way. As a result, eighteen of the forty-four states that offer some form of concealed-carry permit do not recognize permits from any states but their own. Republican representative Cliff Stearns of Florida has sponsored several bills to create a national carrying standard that would allow any person with a valid carrying permit issued by one state to carry a firearm in any other state. In states that did not issue carry permits, a federal

Because there are no federal laws governing concealed weapons, states are forced to address the issue. In Madison, Wisconsin, in 2003, state senator David Zien (right) addresses a group of concealed gun supporters.

standard would permit carrying in public places. A valid concealed-carry permit from someone's home state would then be good in any other state. Although the bills' sponsors insist that carrying a concealed weapon is a fundamental American right, this type of bill has yet to make headway in Congress.

As a result of this lack of a national standard, CCW laws are left entirely up to each individual state and vary considerably from state to state. In 2003, four states (Illinois, Kansas, Nebraska, and Ohio) and Washington, D.C., still prohibited the carrying of concealed weapons under any circumstances. Most states, however, allow their citizens to carry a concealed gun as long as they get a permit from the proper law enforcement authorities. These state CCW laws state the conditions, if any, that would allow a person to carry a concealed firearm in public. In 2003, Alaska and Vermont were the only states that allowed their residents to carry concealed weapons without any permit at all.

States that issue CCW permits can usually be divided into "shall-issue" or "may-issue" states. In shall-issue states, the police are required to give a CCW permit to anyone who meets certain minimal requirements, in the same way that driver's licenses are issued by the state. Once the permit has been issued, the holder is allowed to carry a loaded, concealed firearm in public places such as streets, parks, sports stadiums, bars, and shopping centers (although some state laws do not allow concealed weapons in government buildings). As of 2003, more than thirty states were shall-issue states, including Arizona, Florida, Michigan, North Carolina, Texas, and Pennsylvania. In most cases, it is relatively easy for citizens to get permits in these states; a gun license may be denied only for a clearly defined reason, such as a personal history of crime, alcoholism, insanity, or drug abuse. In 2003, more than 60 percent of Americans and handgun owners lived in shall-issue states, although the number of permit holders varies widely by state; there are 800,000 permits in Florida,

130,000 in Tennessee, 70,000 in Kentucky, and 10,000 in Wyoming.

Fewer than ten states were may-issue states in 2003, but they included some of the nation's most populated states, such as California and New York. In those states, law enforcement officials retain considerable leeway in deciding whether or not to issue CCW permits. Usually, a permit is granted only to people who can show a clear reason why they need to carry a concealed weapon, although there is a big difference in how "clear" is interpreted from case to case, and the process usually favors the wealthy. The permitting process varies greatly from state to state and can be extremely restrictive in some places, such as many counties in California.

In states that adopted shall-issue policies, typically about 1 percent to 2 percent of the eligible population requested a permit. According to one study in the 1990s, approximately 7 percent of adults, or more than 3 million Americans, carry firearms on a regular basis and for reasons not related to their work. Of this total, almost a quarter carry their weapons every day and one-tenth more carry them at least half the time. If these numbers are accurate, almost a million people carry concealed firearms on their person on a typical day.

The Case of Missouri

In 1875, Missouri joined most of the other states in making it illegal to carry concealed weapons. CCW laws were not an issue until the 1980s, when many citizens expressed a desire to change the law. The CCW issue divided Missouri's citizens; rural residents overwhelmingly supported the carrying of concealed guns, while urban voters in Kansas City and St. Louis fought against them at every turn, despite the rising crime rate.

In 1999, CCW supporters placed an initiative on the ballot to repeal Missouri's concealed weapons ban. A bipartisan coalition of law enforcement officials, business leaders, and religious, medical, and community activists

State senator Joan Bray argues against a concealed gun bill in Jefferson City, Missouri, in 2003. The concealed weapon bill sparked a vigorous debate and animosity among the voting public and lawmakers.

organized a strong campaign to defeat the hidden handgun measure. The initiative was defeated by a moderate margin, 53 percent to 48 percent. Nearly every one of Missouri's rural counties voted for the repeal, whereas city residents were overwhelmingly against the initiative. The election was decided by turnout in suburban St. Louis County, a Republican stronghold, where the margin was a surprising 70 percent to 30 percent against the proposal. The national media considered the outcome a defeat for the NRA, which had spent almost $4 million in an effort to get the repeal passed.

Although voters rejected the CCW law, the Missouri legislature defied public opinion by passing a similar bill in 2003. The law would allow Missouri residents who are at least twenty-three years old to apply to their county sheriffs for concealed-carry permits. To be approved, they would have to pass criminal background checks and take an eight-hour safety and marksmanship course. In addition, anyone aged twenty-one and older would be

FAST FACT

Republican representative Frank Barnitz of Missouri said in 2003 that people who don't want to carry guns shouldn't stand in the way of people who desire to carry guns. The legislator said, "We're not asking everyone to carry a concealed weapon. This [the concealed-carry proposal] just lets people who want to carry exercise that right."

able to conceal guns in the glove compartment of a vehicle without a permit. The law did not allow for the release of the names of those who acquired concealed-carry permits. CCW holders would not be permitted to carry guns into Missouri churches, schools, day care centers, or police stations. Amazingly, the new bill was even less restrictive and would require less training than the concealed weapons proposal that Missouri voters had rejected in 1999. In its defense, Republican representative Charles Portwood said, "This is a totally different proposal. There is a change of sentiment. People feel a little bit differently after the United States was attacked [in September 2001]."

When Democratic governor Bob Holden vetoed the concealed-carry proposal, the Republican-dominated legislature overrode the veto in a wild legislative session. One state senator rushed home from his army post in Cuba just in time to cast the deciding vote. The state house of representatives voted 115 to 45 to override, with the state senate narrowly following suit by a 23 to 10 vote that barely cleared the two-thirds majority necessary to override a gubernatorial veto. So despite the 1999 referendum, Missouri became the forty-fifth state to allow some form of citizen ownership of concealed weapons in public in 2003.

CCW Laws:
Arguments, Pro and Con

The firearms industry and gun control opponents pressed for the passage of CCW laws in the 1980s and 1990s. They argued that if more law-abiding citizens carried weapons, lawbreakers would potentially be confronted with more and more armed victims. Criminals would be less likely to attack and rob people because they would never know if their prospective target carried a concealed gun. This would lead to a reduction in crime. CCW supporters noted that the nation's violent crime rate has decreased every year since 1991 and, in 2002, hit a twenty-three-year low.

In the same period, seventeen states adopted and thirteen states improved CCW laws. States with shall-issue CCW laws have lower violent crime rates, on average: 24 percent lower total violent crime, 22 percent lower murder rates, 37 percent lower robbery rates, and 20 percent lower aggravated assault rates. The five states with the lowest violent crime rates are all CCW states.

CCW laws are also defended on symbolic grounds. Because gun ownership is legal in the United States, and the right to defend oneself is presumed, supporters of CCW laws argue that the ability of a law-abiding citizen to carry a weapon in any way should not be restricted. Gun advocate Gary Kleck stated that the idea "that citizens can depend on the police for effective protection is clearly erroneous." He claimed that "robbery and assault victims who used a gun to resist were less likely to

Minnesota, a state that allows citizens to carry concealed weapons, is aggressive about educating and training those who wish to carry firearms. In this photograph, instructor Mike Wolbrink of Plus P Technology (right) shows Joe Fucile a technique for shooting using a wooden dummy gun.

be attacked or to suffer an injury than those who used any other methods of self-protection or those who did not resist at all."

Supporters of CCW laws generally believe that the world can be divided into decent citizens and criminals, into "good guys" and "bad guys." If this worldview is correct, then guns in the right hands can shoot the right people. One woman who supported CCW laws in Texas noted that she might have fought constantly with her boyfriend in a house full of guns, but "never once did it occur to either one of us, ever, to go near the gun during an argument. Because we're not criminals.... The people that you see grabbing a gun in the middle of an argument and shooting each other, they're already criminals. They already have a criminal record.... The people who are out there committing crimes are not the concealed-carry permit holders."

In Michigan, a new state law enacted in 2001 makes it easier to get a concealed weapons permit. Handgun sales have increased in the state since that law went into effect.

While supporters of CCW laws divide the world into felons and law-abiding citizens, with the latter responsible enough to carry loaded weapons in public places, opponents are not so sure. They feel that all people are capable of acting irrationally at times of stress, even to the point of murder: a husband who discovers that his wife wants to leave him; an enraged student or worker with a complaint or a grudge; or anyone under the influence of drugs or alcohol. Women, especially, are more likely to be more threatened by the people that they know than by predatory strangers on the street. Opponents of CCW laws feel that the more people have widespread and immediate access to concealed and loaded handguns, the greater the risk that an otherwise harmless incident, such as a fender bender, might lead to flaring tempers and a fight involving guns. More guns in public might also result in more accidents, especially if inexperienced citizens begin using guns without any real justification.

Opponents also argue that the checks on who receives CCW permits in shall-issue states are not effective. According to one study of Texas's CCW law by the anti-gun advocates at the Violence Policy Center, between January 1, 1996, and April 30, 2000, holders of concealed handgun licenses in Texas were arrested for 3,370 crimes, including murder, rape, kidnapping, and theft. Since the law was adopted, license holders had been arrested for more than two crimes per day, more than three drunk driving offenses per week, and weapons-related crimes at a rate two-thirds higher than that of Texas's overall population. Former Texas governor Ann Richards, an opponent of CCW laws, stated that men told her that they didn't want CCW legislation for themselves, but "'for my wife, girlfriend, daughter'…whatever other female you could name. But the reverse was true among the women who came to see me. They said, 'For God's sake, do not let these men carry concealed weapons.'"

FAST FACT

In September 2003, a would-be robber in Utah received quite a surprise. When he entered a Provo bus station and handed the clerk a note demanding money, the clerk, a concealed weapons permit holder, took the robbery suspect into custody at gunpoint.

CCW and Self-Defense

The symbolic issues involved in supporting or opposing CCW laws probably cannot be resolved, because they speak to deeply held beliefs of Americans regarding the Constitution, government, and people of the United States. The practical question of whether CCW laws reduce crime or lead to an increase in successful self-defense uses of handguns, however, may be answerable. Once again, it hinges on how often Americans use their weapons in self-defense.

Officially justifiable homicides are extremely rare in the United States, averaging only 176 per year for the five years between 1997 and 2001. This is less than 2 percent of all recorded homicides in the United States. This seemed to imply that CCW laws would have a limited effect on the American crime rate. However, in 1997, authors John Lott and David Mustard published a study claiming that the rate of person-against-person crimes decreased significantly in states that passed shall-issue CCW laws. The writers stated, "We find that allowing citizens to carry concealed weapons deters violent crimes and it appears to produce no increase in accidental deaths." Lott repeated this claim the next year in his book *More Guns, Less Crime.* Traveling around the United States, Lott testified at political hearings to assist the passage of concealed-carry laws. Lott asserted, "Guns are used for defensive purposes about five times as often as they are used for crimes."

Counterstudies quickly followed. In an article in 1999, Daniel Webster and Jens Ludwig discussed "the many limitations of Lott's and Gary Kleck's research," especially the small, self-reporting sample and the unreliability of the respondents. In one of Kleck's surveys, only 56 out of 5,000 respondents (about 1 percent) reported that they had used a gun in self-defense during the last year; each report therefore represented about 50,000 defensive gun uses. For that reason, the smallest change in the answers of a few

FAST FACT

Even experienced gun users sometimes make fatal mistakes. In 2002, a police officer in Tennessee was shot to death by his three-year-old son. The officer had just arrived home, placed his service weapon on the kitchen table, and turned to greet his pregnant wife. His three-year-old picked up the gun and, thinking it was a toy, fired one shot into his father's back, killing him. The tragedy was heightened by the fact that the officer had taken a home-firearms safety course before he was issued his weapon.

respondents would lead to enormous differences in the total. Webster and Ludwig asserted that "the best science indicates that more guns will lead to more deaths." In 2003, John Donohue, in another study that examined U.S. crime statistics, described Lott's work as "deeply flawed" and "misguided." Donohue concluded, "If somebody had to say which way the evidence is stronger, I'd say that it's probably stronger that the [CCW] laws are increasing crime, rather than decreasing crime."

Despite training and education for those who obtain concealed weapons permits, there is always room for error. Many researchers point out that human beings can make mistakes when taken by surprise, as the subject in this photograph might have been when awakened by a sound in the middle of the night.

The Second Amendment Sisters marched in opposition to the Million Mom March in Washington, D.C., on May 14, 2000. The former group favors gun education, while the latter favors stricter gun laws.

Nonetheless, Lott's work had a much greater impact than that of his opponents. The phrase "more guns, less crime" became the slogan of CCW supporters. The publicity from Lott's work may have influenced the passage of CCW laws in several states, including Michigan, Minnesota, and Missouri. Lott testified at the 1999 hearings of the House Judiciary Committee after the

murders at Columbine High School. His address to the committee, titled "Gun Regulations Can Cost Lives," strongly argued that gun control laws "will actually increase the amount of harm suffered by good citizens" and that everyone would be safer if even more Americans carried guns.

The Mysterious Survey

In his published work, Lott claimed that concealed handguns deterred crime without being fired an astoundingly high 98 percent of the time. That claim allowed Lott to explain away the fact that extremely few self-defense uses of handguns were ever reported and that U.S. hospital emergency rooms were not swamped with wounded criminals. At the time, nine other published surveys had produced numbers ranging from 21 percent to 67 percent for how often Americans actually had to fire their guns in self-defense—far more than the 2 percent claimed by Lott. When scholars began questioning the manner in which Lott had derived this percentage, Lott changed his story several times, attributing the number to "national surveys" and then some particular polls. In 2000, Lott asserted that the "98 percent" came from his own survey, but his computer had crashed and he had lost all the data. According to Lott, he funded the survey himself and used unknown students to make the survey calls (although no records of this exist at all). Lott now faces questions about whether he fabricated the entire survey, raising serious doubts about his ethics and credibility.

The case of John Lott was somewhat similar to the fall of Michael Bellesiles, the disgraced historian who engaged in questionable research standards to support his anti-gun book, *Arming America*. The book, which dealt with the history of firearms in American culture, claimed that guns were not nearly as common in the 1700s and early 1800s as previously believed. Bellesiles's book received, and then was stripped of, the prestigious Bancroft Prize in history

> **FAST FACT**
>
> In February 2003, John Lott confessed that for at least three years, he had repeatedly taken on the made-up identity of a former student of his, whom he named "Mary Rosh" in online arguments. Under this false identity, he unashamedly praised his own book, scholarship, and impartiality. Not surprisingly, Mary Rosh thought that John Lott was a superb professor; Lott wrote about himself: "I have to say that he was the best professor that I ever had."

Many small-business owners protect themselves and their livelihoods with firearms. Richard Rhee holds an AK-47, one of about thirty-five weapons he has on hand to protect the five grocery stores he owns in the Los Angeles area.

for 2002. Like Lott, Bellesiles continues to insist that his political and philosophical opponents cause all his troubles.

However, Lott's difficulties went beyond the mysterious survey. His coauthor, when placed under oath in a court case, admitted that there were serious flaws in their study that could undermine their conclusion about more guns leading to less crime. Lott's study apparently omitted possible variables that could explain that changes in the crime rate were due to reasons other than changes in CCW laws. For example, Lott failed to account for major factors in each state, such as wealth, drug and alcohol use, and police practices such as community policing. Even Gary Kleck found that Lott's findings regarding the reductions in crime after CCW laws were passed were probably inaccurate. Kleck wrote, "More likely, the declines in crime coinciding with relaxation of carry laws were largely attributable to other factors not controlled in the Lott and Mustard analysis."

The Triumph of State CCW Laws

Although the research on the effectiveness of CCW laws in reducing crime is greatly disputed, the general national trend is clear. Forty-five states now offer some version of CCW permits, with the great majority of these being shall-issue states. Some popular Web sites now offer tips on learning how to carry a concealed weapon legally.

The confusion of Americans over the desirability of gun regulations in the United States is evident from actions taken in the 1990s and early 2000s on the state and national levels. On one hand, there are new laws restricting firearms possession and usage (background checks, assault weapons bans), while on the other, there is a considerable level of gun decontrol, such as the passage of CCW laws.

Statistics will probably not decide the CCW issue or, indeed, any issue involving firearms regulations in the United States, because the debate over gun use in America long ago entered the symbolic realm. In the United States, opposition has often developed whenever the

> **FAST FACT**
>
> CCW laws can also be a source of controversy if they place unreasonable requirements on private organizations that want to ban handguns from private property. For example, since the terrorist attacks in 2001, many Americans are leery of armed citizens in public places such as sports stadiums. In Minnesota in 2003, churches and other religious organizations challenged a new state CCW law that prohibited them from banning guns from their private parking lots. The case is still in the courts.

government—national, state, or local—has attempted to regulate individual behavior in the name of "the public good." As long as gun owners view the right to carry concealed and loaded weapons in public as a "freedom" issue and gun control opponents see it as a "public good" issue, some form of the debate will continue.

CHAPTER 6

The Unending Debate

The United States boasts one of the highest standards of living in the world but it also has extremely high levels of gun violence. In 2000, firearms injuries ranked second (behind automobile accidents) as the leading cause of injury deaths, killing 28,663 Americans. Approximately 58 percent of these deaths were suicides, but that left more than 16,000 people who were killed with firearms, including about 700 who died in gun accidents. Between 1993 and 2001, victims faced offenders armed with guns in about 27 percent of robberies, 8 percent of assaults, and 3 percent of sexual assaults.

If restricting gun usage and ownership could be proven to reduce the murder rate, then many more Americans would support this type of legislation. However, many gun advocates have made the intellectual argument that the Second Amendment gives Americans a constitutional right to bear arms and that these armed citizens are the basic building block of American freedom. Gun advocates also take a more pragmatic approach, claiming that individual and private firearms ownership serves a crucial purpose in individual self-defense and in reducing the crime rate. In their view, gun control legislation would not reduce violence in America but would actually increase it. This is an absolutely crucial claim; is it possible to test it?

Because the death of thousands of Americans each year is obviously a public health issue, the Centers for Disease Control and Prevention (CDC) became involved in the gun issue. The CDC, headquartered in Atlanta, Georgia, is a federal agency associated with the Department of Health and Human Services. Its mission is to promote health and quality of life, both in the United States and abroad, by preventing and controlling disease, injury, and disability.

In the early years of the twenty-first century, the CDC began a sweeping review of the nation's gun control laws. A group of scientists reviewed fifty-one published studies about the effectiveness of eight different types of control

FAST FACT

In 1993, the head of the CDC noted, "Anything we can do to get guns out of the hands of children and out of homes would reduce the fatality rate. They may still fight, but they'll do it like we did, with fists and not guns." Gun advocates claim that statements like this show the CDC is biased against gun ownership. Since 1996, the U.S. Congress has specifically prohibited the CDC from using any funds "to advocate or promote gun control."

regulations, including legislation banning specific firearms or ammunition, barring felons from buying guns, and requiring waiting periods or gun registration. All of the studies that they examined were private; none were by the federal government.

In October 2003, the CDC released its findings, if they can be called that. In every case of gun control legislation, the CDC task force found "insufficient evidence to

Young people may receive mixed messages about guns with the proliferation of video games simulating gunplay. At an NRA convention in 1998, Tyler Robinson of New Jersey tried out a virtual reality target practice game.

After states pass laws favoring the carrying of concealed weapons, there is always a rise in gun sales.

determine effectiveness." There were so many potential variables to consider in the rise and fall of the crime rate that the scientists and statisticians found it impossible to draw any meaningful conclusions. Even such common-sense and widely supported measures as restricting gun

ownership by former criminals could not conclusively be shown to have had any effect on the crime rate.

Gun Regulation as a Symbolic Issue

When the Constitution was written in 1787, America was a preindustrial society. Goods were made by hand, transportation depended on animals and the wind, and most people were farmers. There were no electric lights, cars, computers, televisions, chain stores, or mass production. In 1790, Philadelphia, Pennsylvania, was the largest city in the United States, with a population of 42,000 people; Salem and Marblehead, Massachusetts, and Portsmouth, New Hampshire, were all ranked in the top ten cities in the nation by population.

How far away that world seems from modern, industrialized, urban, and bureaucratic American society! Fewer and fewer people work for themselves or even for an employer whom they know; many work for enormous, faceless corporations. The American economy is tied to a vast world economy; people's jobs depend on things that they can hardly control, such as oil production and currency exchange rates in faraway places. Life in a free market society is extremely competitive, and in any competition, some people win and some lose. In America, advertising teaches people that they should be able to have whatever they want, but only if they can pay for it, and if they can't, they're unsuccessful. Some people in distant nations hate the United States and its policies so much that they're willing to carry out massive acts of destruction with no regard for the loss of the lives of innocent citizens.

Against this background, guns provide power, authority, and a sense of mastery. With a gun, the smallest, weakest, and poorest feel that they stand equal to the biggest, strongest, and richest. As a machine, a gun is relatively simple and has hardly changed over the last two centuries. In a confusing world, a gun is straightforward yet also magical; it contains within it the power of life and death. For many Americans—especially

FAST FACT

FAST FACT

On September 15, 2001, a three-year-old Spotsylvania County, Virginia, boy shot and killed himself with a gun that his father said he had "brought into the house for protection after the terrorist attacks" on September 11. For no apparent reason, the father had hung the semiautomatic pistol in its holster from a curtain rod in the boy's bedroom.

men—the acquisition of their first gun is a rite of passage, a clear physical sign that one has reached adulthood. It's not surprising that handgun sales soared immediately after the terrorist attacks on September 11, 2001; the owner of a gun, at least, commands respect, and carrying a gun gives an individual a sense of security, even if a handgun is unlikely to shoot down airplanes from the sky.

On the other hand, many people do not desire firearms for such a "magical" power. Millions of pragmatic American gun owners want firearms for practical self-defense for themselves and their families. One pro-gun advocate noted,

> People want guns after September 11...[because the terrorist attacks that day] reminded them that order and police protection are fragile and uncertain. The next September 11 may lead to a blackout and police absence. Who will then protect my family and me, not against terrorists, but against local criminals who see an opportunity? The police won't, just as they failed to protect so many in the 1992 Los Angeles riots. My gun, on the other hand, might help protect me.

The passion that people bring to the debate over the place of guns in the United States makes compromise almost impossible. Supporters and opponents of gun control might argue all day long whether this or that regulation has affected the crime rate, but in the end, the symbolic issues may appear to trump the practical ones. For example, analysis of the two phrases of the Second Amendment ("A well regulated militia, being necessary to the security of a free State, the right of the people to keep and bear arms, shall not be infringed.") often rests upon an appeal to history. Opponents of gun control emphasize the individualistic character of the founders of the United States, while supporters of gun regulations keep insisting that the founders were more concerned with the collective behavior of Americans. There is no shortage of evidence to support both positions.

Parents often pass their views on guns and gun ownership on to their children. The young girl holding a gun in this photograph is the daughter of a member of Second Amendment Sisters.

A family stages a protest against the Million Mom March in Washington, D.C., in 2000.

However, in most ways, this historical argument only acts to camouflage much deeper issues. An American's position on gun ownership and gun control is related to a host of deeply held beliefs regarding the meaning of the Constitution, the effectiveness of the government, the strengths and weaknesses of democracy, and the intelligence and trustworthiness of the people of the United States. These are not issues that can be easily settled by resorting to statistics, anecdotes, or history. In the end, even popular opinion has its limits. As Henry David Thoreau noted in the opening chapter of his classic *Walden* in 1854, "Public opinion is a weak tyrant compared with our own private opinion. What a man thinks of himself, that is which determines, or rather, indicates, his fate."

No End in Sight

The conceptual argument over the place of guns in America is probably unsolvable. One of the tests of a logical position—a position held on evidence, as opposed to a belief based upon faith (such as belief in God)—is whether *any* proof could ever shake a person from his or her point of view. Gun control supporters and gun advocates often claim to be able to see each other's points of view, but the terms of the debate seem to imply otherwise. There is probably no evidence that could ever be presented that would convince a gun advocate that firearms are not a necessity to preserve American freedom and allow for effective individual self-defense. Likewise, until the unlikely event that the firearms death and injury rate approaches zero, gun control supporters will continue to believe that guns in the United States require stricter regulation.

However, human beings exist in a real, and not a theoretical, world. The United States is a representative democracy that tries to practice the creed of "majority rules, minority rights." On an issue like gun regulation, where opinions are fixed and both sides boast millions of followers, a certain amount of compromise is inevitable, especially in the making of laws. This need for compromise in the real world explains the extraordinarily wide range of gun regulation across the United States. It also seems to imply that the debate over the place of guns in American life will continue for the foreseeable future.

Glossary

advocacy group—an organization that seeks to persuade people to support a particular viewpoint on a public issue, such as for or against increased restrictions on gun use

amendment—a change or addition to a legal document, such as an amendment to the U.S. Constitution

armory—a place where arms are manufactured

assault weapons—antipersonnel rifles, shotguns, and handguns designed mainly for military and law enforcement purposes

caliber—a measurement of the inside of a gun barrel

commerce clause—a clause in the U.S. Constitution that empowers Congress to act in matters involving trade between the states

crime rate—the amount of crime, presented in statistical terms

firearm—a weapon that uses a powder charge to shoot something, usually a bullet or shell, from a straight tube

gun control—restrictions on the use and ownership of guns

homicide—murder

inalienable right—a fundamental right that cannot be taken away

individual right—a right held by the people as individuals

justifiable homicide—the killing of a person by another person to prevent a felony, which the law considers legally permissible

legal immunity—protection from legal responsibility

liability—legal obligation or responsibility

magazine—the container in a firearm that stores the cartridges before they pass into the chamber for firing

militia—a military organization made up of people who are not professional soldiers

police power—the power of a government to preserve public order and maintain minimum standards of health, safety, and welfare for its citizens

poll—a sampling of public opinion

preemption—a legal doctrine allowing the federal government to take away a state's right to make laws on a certain topic

school zone—as designated by law, a geographic area around a school in which firearms are strictly regulated

self-defense—an action by an individual to protect himself or herself

semiautomatic weapon—a weapon that reloads automatically after firing, although the trigger must be pulled to fire each round; different from an automatic weapon, which fires more than one round with a single pull of the trigger

suicide—the taking of one's own life

trigger lock—a device incorporated into a firearm to prevent its accidental firing

waiting period—a period of time before a person takes possession of a gun after purchase, during which background checks can be performed

Bibliography

Books

Blumstein, Alfred, and Joel Wallman, eds. *The Crime Drop in America.* Cambridge, UK: Cambridge University Press, 2000.

Dizard, Jan, et al. *Guns in America: A Reader.* New York: New York University Press, 1999.

Kleck, Gary. *Targeting Guns: Firearms and Their Control.* New York: Aldine de Gruyter, 1997.

Roleff, Tamara. *Guns and Crime.* San Diego: Greenhaven, 2000.

Spitzer, Robert. *The Politics of Gun Control.* 2nd ed. New York: Chatham House, 1998.

Utter, Glenn. *Encyclopedia of Gun Control and Gun Rights.* Phoenix: Oryx Press, 2000.

Webster, Daniel, and Jens Ludwig. *Myths about Defensive Gun Use and Permissive Gun Carry Laws.* Berkeley, CA: Media Studies Group, 2000.

Web Sites

The Brady Campaign to Prevent Gun Violence United with the Million Mom March *www.handguncontrol.org*

Centers for Disease Control and Prevention (CDC) National Center for Injury Prevention and Control (NCIPC)—Fatal Injuries: Mortality Reports *webapp.cdc.gov/sasweb/ncipc/mortrate.html*

Firearms Law Center *www.firearmslawcenter.org/content/home.asp*

National Rifle Association (NRA) *www.nra.org*

Packing.org—Home of the CCW Database *www.packing.org*

United States Department of Justice—Bureau of Justice Statistics (BJS) *www.ojp.usdoj.gov/bjs/welcome.html*

Index

Note: Page numbers in *italics* indicate illustrations and captions.